The NEW CRYSTAL CODES

**ALIGN Your CRYSTALS
To The New Energies**

*Crystal Codes, Ciphers and Functions
For the New Era
Recognise a Record-Keeper, an Isis and more*

MYRA SRI

Energy Healing Secrets Series; 4

COPYRIGHT and LEGAL NOTICE

This Book is Copyright © 2015 and Beyond: Myra Sri (the 'Author'). All rights reserved worldwide.

Reproduction or translation of any part of this work beyond that permitted by section 107 or 108 of the 1976 United States Copyright Act without permission of the copyright owner is unlawful. Requests for permission or further information should be addressed to the Author. No part of this eBook may be translated or reproduced or transmitted in any form or by any means, electronic or mechanical, including photocopying, recording, or by an information storage and retrieval system without the express permission of the Author.

This publication is designed to provide accurate and Authoritative information in regard to the subject matter covered, based on the Author's experience, research, practice and understandings. The Author and publisher do not recommend anything contrary to common sense. If professional medical or nutritional advice or other expert assistance is required, the services of a competent professional person should be sought.

First Published as an electronic book in Australia 2015
First Printing, **April 2017**
ISBN: 9780992392444
Published by Healing Knowhow Publishing,
P.O.Box 126, Toukley, NSW 2263

National Library of Australia Cataloguing-in-Publication entry:
Sri, Myra, author
The new crystal codes - align your crystals to the new
energies : crystal codes, ciphers and
functions for the new era, new: align your
crystals, choosing and working with
crystals / Myra Sri
ISBN: 9780992392444 (paperback)
Energy healing secrets series ; 4
Crystals--Therapeutic use
Energy medicine
133.2548

Acknowledgements

Thank you to my clients, students and colleagues for your encouragement.

Blessed be the gifts of Nature, the gifts of Light and the gifts of Gaia. And Blessings to all those who seek more of the Light.

Contents

- **INTRODUCTION** 9
- **THE NEW CRYSTAL ERA** 13
  - WHY CRYSTALS NEED RE-ALIGNMENT 17
    - Crystal Effectiveness 19
    - How to Use a Pendulum 20
    - Testing the Crystal 22
- **EVOLUTION** 23
  - CRYSTAL BACKGROUND 25
    - How Crystals Grow 25
  - CRYSTAL FORMATIONS 26
  - HOW CRYSTALS WORK 27
- **CARING FOR CRYSTALS** 29
  - Selecting Your Crystal 29
  - Crystals That Never Need Cleaning 30
  - Crystals That Clean Other Crystals 31
  - Wearing Crystals 31
  - Using and Working with Crystals 32
  - Intention - Centering Ones Self 33
- **CRYSTAL CLEANING** 35
  - Cleaning vs Clearing Crystals 35
  - Crystals To Keep Dry 37
  - 1. CLEANING: 38
  - 2. CLEARING 40
  - 3. PROGRAMMING CRYSTALS 43
    - No 1 – The Breathe and 'Intention' 44
    - No 2 – Visualisation 44
    - No 3 – Breathe and Both Hands 46
    - No 4 - Third Eye Program 46

    No 5 - For Self Use.. 47
    No 6 – For Use with Others 48
  4. MAINTENANCE 50
    For Healers... 51
    Charging Crystals 51

CRYSTAL HEALING 53
  Trauma or Shock 53
  Normal Sessions 55

QUARTZ POWER 56
  QUARTZ - Rock Crystal... 57
  CHANNELING CRYSTAL – 7 sides............................. 60
  CRYSTALS WITH BABIES... 62
  DOUBLE TERMINATED CRYSTALS $\updownarrow$ 63
  ELESTIALS QUARTZ CRYSTALS............................... 64
  FADEN CRYSTAL 66
  ISIS CRYSTALS – 5 sides.. 67
  GROUNDING CRYSTALS – 8 sides 68
  LEMURIAN QUARTZ CRYSTALS 70
  QUARTZ CLUSTERS 71
  AMETHYST/SMOKEY CLUSTERS............................ 71
  RAINBOW CRYSTALS.. 72
  RECORD KEEPERS ▲ 73
  SELF-HEALED and PHANTOM CRYSTALS 74
  TRIGGER CRYSTALS 74
  TWIN CRYSTALS II 75
  WINDOW CRYSTALS ◊ 76

CRYSTAL SETS 78
  Crystal Set for Love 79
  Crystal Set for Protection 81
  Crystal Set for Stress Relief...................................... 83

Crystal Set for Success 85

45 Crystals - Quick Reference 87

1. Amazonite 89
2. Amethyst 92
3. Apophyllite Pyramids 95
4. Aquamarine 97
5. Aragonite 100
6. Atacamite 103
7. Aventurine 105
8. Azeztulite 107
9. Black Onyx 109
10. Black Tourmaline 111
11. Blue Lace Agate 113
12. Boji Stones 115
13. Botswana Agate 118
14. Calcite 121
15. Carnelian 124
16. Cerussite 126
17. Chevron Amethyst 128
18. Citrine 130
19. Clear Quartz Crystal 133
20. Danburite 134
21. Dendritic Agate 137
22. Dumortierite (Blue quartz) 140
23. Fire Agate 143
24. Hematite 145
25. Labradorite 147
26. Lapis Lazuli 150
27. Lepidolite 153
28. Morganite (Pink Beryl) 155
29. Onyx 158

30. Pink ManganoCalcite (Pink Calcite) 160
31. Rhodochrosite 162
32. Rose Quartz 165
33. Rubellite (Pink or Red Tourmaline) 167
34. Ruby 170
35. Rutilated Quartz 173
36. Smoky Quartz 175
37. Snowflake Obsidian 179
38. Star Sapphire 181
39. Sunstone 184
40. Tigers Eye 187
41. Topaz 190
42. Tourmaline 193
43. Turquoise 196
44. Verdelite (Green Tourmaline) 200
45. Yellow Jasper 203

THE NEW CRYSTAL CODES 207

EVOLVING CRYSTALS 207
WHAT ARE THE CRYSTAL CODES? 209
COLOR FREQUENCIES — COLOR CODES 211
Crystal Colour Codes 213

CRYSTAL CIPHER CODES 215

Activation Code 216
Consciousness Code 216
Creation Code 216
Dormant Code 217
Dream Code 217
Earth History Code 217
Evolutionary Code 218
Genetic / DNA Code 218

- Healing Code 218
- Instruction Code 219
- Planetary System Code 219
- Programming Code 220
- StarSeed Code 220
- Synchronisation Code 220
- Transformation Code 221
- Transmission Code 221
- Accessing the Cipher Code 222

THE ALIGNMENT PROCESS 223

ALIGNMENT PROCESS FOR CRYSTALS 225

SIMPLE SELF ALIGNMENT FIRST 225
- Prepare to Align 225
- Establish the Current Energies 226
- Alignment to the New Energies 227
- Activation of the New Energies 228
- Notes on the Process 228

ALIGNING AND ACTIVATING YOUR CRYSTALS 229

THE NEW ENERGY WAVES 233
WHAT IS 'THE NEW ENERGY WAVE' 233

WHERE TO NEXT? 235
- Evolving Chakras 235
- FURTHER INFORMATION 239
- ABOUT THE AUTHOR 241

Introduction

As a young girl, I was amazed with the crystal formations that I saw in the caves of England and Wales viewed during school trips. They made an impression on me. In more recent years, and in particular since the early 1990's, my interest has been renewed afresh.

The remarkable thing about crystals is that even though they are incredible examples of nature and her forces and beauty, they are also in very common and everyday use; in watches, ultrasound machines and other devices. Computer screens cannot operate without crystals and crystal technology. I also remember my father having a radio in his garden shed. It used a quartz crystal and a cat's whisker (as it was called) to tune in to radio stations. I got into trouble for adjusting the dial to hear the various stations that it reached, so caught up with it that I had forgotten that touching was forbidden…

Yet many people do not acknowledge the presence of crystals, and worse, decry their abilities and sneer at the mention of the word.

These earth stones can be viewed on a physical level as things of beauty or adornment, but they are valuable on many more levels. Their vibrational actions are always consistent and they really are amazing bundles of minerals, molecules and power atoms that are geared to assist mankind and to enrich the earth.

Many of you are already aware that we are journeying through new energies towards a new age. Some have called this coming time as an age of Enlightenment, others see it as an Ascension process, and yet others see it as a change in Global and Human Consciousness.

However you perceive it, it is an exciting time.

As we travel and spiral through the Cosmos, our planet orbiting around our own Sun, which in turn is travelling and spiraling around the Central Sun of Alcyone, which in itself is travelling and spiraling around another yet greater Central Sun, we pass through new energies, new cosmic geolocations, new galactic longitudes and latitudes in the space-grid matrix.

Our view from this planet changes little, but our position in space actually changes a lot... and along the way we encounter new frequencies.

These new frequencies impact on our existing energy bodies, on our consciousness and perceptions in a new and entirely different way and they also vibrationally impact on a whole new range of fresh frequencies on this planet in a whole new way. They create ripples, if you like, of new incoming vibrations and resonances that can and do activate us in many ways.

I have worked with crystals for over thirty years and have discovered that their energies have shifted and changed, just as many of us on this Planet have undergone our own shifts and personal evolution, especially in the last twenty years or so. I share my knowledge with you of how to re-align your crystals with the new Era energies.

You will not find this knowledge anywhere else yet.

You will also hopefully find in these pages more ways that will enhance your understanding of crystals, and safe ways to clean and care for them as well as how to tell how they are working for you. You don't need to be a psychic or sensitive to be able to do so. Anyone can use these methods, and they are quick, safe and easy.

You will also learn: how to identify the various functions of crystals; some metaphysical properties; sets of crystals; and learn the difference between an Isis crystal, a Record-Keeper, a Lemurian and much more...

Make the most of your willing crystal and harness its energies for the new energy shifts right now!

Treat them with love, care and wisdom. Respect them, and they will become your friends!

CLUSTER

THE NEW CRYSTAL ERA

Evolution of Consciousness in Nature is happening right now. I have seen and felt it with Essential Oils, as well as with some of the ancient ways of doing things, ancient healing energies and modalities. Some methods that used to work seemed to stop working and new ways and techniques or new applications of them seemed to be required to "break through" to the next level – or stagnation might occur.

The planet herself is the creator of our Crystals – through processes of heat, pressure, eruption, water distillation, hypothermia, and an awesome and complicated system of interplay between the planet and the elements. We are all experiencing the new energies through our constant shifts in what I call the cosmic longitude and latitudinal geolocation changes as we spiral through the Cosmos on our journey aboard Planet Earth. So too are the Crystals and all of nature's creations.

We, as well as our Planet, are undergoing a process of evolution – in humanity, in nature, in consciousness. This not only includes our attitudes to the planet, but also to our food sources, to our health and our way of life. These energy shifts in consciousness are affecting many and are also affecting attitudes to the traditional and natural therapies. There is more awareness taking place as to what we put in our mouths, in our food, on our bodies. The new frequencies are affecting everything – and this includes our light pulsating Crystals as well as our beloved Essential Oils.

I have already written about the evolution of Essential Oils through the incoming new energies and of how we can enhance our existing use of them and their etheric actions and unseen etheric colour codes. (*"Secrets Beyond Aromatherapy"*.)

So too have Crystals evolved. Their base frequencies have shifted, their potentialities have increased, but they, like us, are oftentimes needing a trigger to align and activate them correctly.

Even though I had been aware of new Chakra anatomy and of the changes in Essential Oils and their abilities, it was mainly by accident that I became aware of how the new frequencies were impacting on Crystals and their energies.

I stumbled upon this understanding when a major crisis occurred. It was after I had been travelling overseas attending to a family crisis and had left all of my belongings in the care of family at home. This included my work tools and crystal collection. An unexpected disaster happened whilst I was away and it looked like I had lost everything, including my precious crystals in a fire. When we later sifted through the debris we discovered some of them still very well packed amongst singed packing and burnt towels in a melted large plastic container. We were able to prise the melted plastic open and rescue some, and so I began to tend and later reactivate my surviving crystals again after the shock they had gone through. They had ceased to work, and I thought I knew why – the assumption being that it was because of the fire and the heat that had actually burnt and destroyed some of them. Some crystals were totally destroyed in the fire, blackened and unable to perform again. After tending for the remaining crystals and checking their energies, I realised that they were still not functioning as I knew and felt that they could. I still assumed it was because of the fire.

But when I started checking other newer crystals I had also begun to obtain whilst I was away, I found that even these also were *all* energetically "stilted". Upon further examination I realised that all of the Crystal energies had been affected by something else. This also corroborated other energetic work I had been doing that involved Planetary energies and the new Earthing Chakra system.

Then I remembered what I had been saying to others; that the energy shifts we were experiencing had impacted us all and that we required an upgrade or alignment to these very frequencies. From this I again realised that the planetary frequencies were still shifting to accommodate the new energies and this was now also being reflected in the crystals, which I hadn't previously considered.

Now I was able to work out that not only my previous crystals but also these other and "newer" crystals required alignment to the new energies as well.

Being aware of this possibility I then tested this theory and also discovered through working with crystals belonging to others that these crystals too were also overcome by the incoming frequencies and the new energy shifts that they simply registered absolutely *nothing*! When tested with the pendulum many of them could not even raise a forward-backward movement – nothing!

They were *not functioning at all*!

This meant that not only did they most certainly require cleaning, but that this was only part of the issue – for underneath that was the fact that they were not yet engaged with the new energies! They were asleep. Just like some people who go asleep when they are challenged and cannot get their heads around something new and so they switch off, so too had these crystals fallen asleep in their energy and consciousness. Cleaning and clearing would NOT be enough to get them lively and happy again!

Here in this book I explain how to align the use of crystals with these new incoming frequencies. I believe that this is very important right now, for if we don't upgrade them with current energetic alignment in order to be able to reprogram and use our crystals to match these new energies, they will continue to work in the same 'old' way and will miss out on converting effectively the new potential energies and transforming abilities that we are currently traversing and experiencing. I also believe that periodically they may require the same process, for we are all on a journey, and as we upgrade other things in life – technology, clothing, phones – periodically, we also may need to upgrade these amazing receptors, utilisers and transmitters of energy.

Crystals have evolved, and right now require a new alignment, a new reordering of their frequencies, a new link-in and connection with humanity, as well as human, planetary, global and cosmic energies.

I give you the system I use here, and I have found that even though I am a fully qualified kinesiology trainer, testing with a pendulum is the easiest and most visual method of confirming the process of alignment. And I include instructions for doing this if you don't already know. But please feel free to work out your own method. The instructions for aligning your crystal, *any* crystal is given in the Chapter on *"Alignment Process for Crystals"*.

This little book has everything you need to identify the different functions and powers of Quartz Crystals and much, much more. We will also look at some of the current information on crystals, including caring for and working with crystals.

You will learn about how to connect to your crystal, how to care for it, code and program it and how to use it wisely.

You will find in these pages ideas that will inspire you to love and journey with your chosen gem and to keep it working for you effectively and efficiently in these current times.

WHY CRYSTALS NEED RE-ALIGNMENT

We live in a sea of energy, and we are all varying frequencies of energy and vibration. Science is now understanding the underlying quantum mechanics and physics that underpin our world.

As we journey through space and the Cosmos we pass through varying frequencies that we have not encountered before. These frequencies can have a variety of effects upon existing vibrational resonances.

To put it simply, the new frequencies require processing.

When they are unfamiliar frequencies this process may take some time, or may require something to assist in aligning with the new frequencies.

Those who are on a spiritual journey may be somewhat more familiar with these shifts in energy, and may often be able to process them more quickly if they have the correct current tools that they need to do so. The average person who is busy keeping their job or a roof over their head, will naturally prioritise things according to their time, values and ability to manage things. But they will still be processing the effects. They may possibly feel more stress, be more challenged, or develop strange aches and pains and even allergies. This does not mean that they are doing anything wrong. This is simply their way of coping.

Awareness and recognition are primary in navigating through the new frequencies without being thrown or overly challenged.

As in music, harmonising is a key to dealing with and harnessing the new frequencies, as some frequencies may be disresonant with certain others, possibly creating a kind of discord or jarring of the pre-existing energies. Not every frequency must match exactly, this is not really always possible, but there can be sets or ranges of frequencies that get along well together. As we move through the new energies and frequencies that are being more intensely received from other Cosmic Solar Systems, we may well need to harmonise ourself with these to feel and function more comfortably and effectively in the new energetic environment.

To cope with the new space-locations and energy wave-bands that we find ourselves in, and also as a result of some of the frequencies we have been experiencing in these last twenty to thirty years or so, many have actually been developing ways of transducing the energies and have evolved in their energetic structure. Just as we require alignment in these new structures and anatomy, so crystals may well require similar alignments.

The new evolved Earthing Chakra system is one such new system of current energetic alignment in the human subtle body anatomy. However, you do not need to know about this to align your crystals. This information is just to explain that there has been a process of development that has occurred to this *Now* point in time and is still going on as we traverse this wave-band of new energies. You will probably have heard about the Mayan Long Count Calendar, which talked about the ending of one age, and the beginning of another. [An age just doesn't simply "click-over" like a number counter, instantly forgetting what was happening before.]

It takes time to engage from a particularly huge or previously all-encompassing energy to fully embrace the energy of another era, and these energies merge and mix the closer they are together. We are very close to the centre of the exact turn-over or "click-over" which takes approximately fifty years or so to kind of "engage" fully. You could almost say that we are not quite there yet, but we are certainly well on our way.

The sensitivity of our crystals can be affected by energetic impact. And we are undergoing energetic impact. Just as the old ways of doing and being are giving way to the new, so the energies of the old ways of doing and being for crystals have also been affected.

To work consciously and effectively with them in these present times will require a consciousness that understands that things have shifted and changed and that we need to harness the new energies to continue to be effective. Aligning your crystals in the way that I share with you later will allow you to harness these new and positive energies more effectively.

You will be provided with full alignment instructions and also pendulum instructions.

Crystal Effectiveness

You can establish if your crystal is available to work for you in a variety of ways. When I use the word "available", it simply means that it is able to work for you and is ready to work.

If it is not charged up and has become exhausted, you may need to know this beforehand.

If it is overwhelmed with toxic energies, it will require cleaning first.

If its energies are not in alignment with the energies that are available for healing and repair, it will not be effective in its efforts.

As mentioned earlier, even though I often use kinesiology and am quite sensitive, I often count on the visual actions of pendulum testing to ensure and establish a good working state and readiness from the crystal.

Asking the crystal to **"Show me now what you are doing"** can reveal its energetic capability in the form of its arc of motion and its speed of motion.

A sludgy type of action from the pendulum can indicate toxicity or tiredness. Whilst a smooth and quickening spiral can indicate the crystal charging itself up and showing it is ready to work.

It used to be that if I tested a wand or a longish shaped crystal and it indicated a forward-backward movement, then this showed by this movement that it was ready to work.

Times have changed, and for me I now know that it is not really ready or aligned to *current* frequencies until it is showing a clockwise circular motion – this I take as indicating its *vortex* action and transforming capabilities.

How to Use a Pendulum

A pendulum is a mechanism that shows energy movement clearly by rotation or movement via a suspended crystal or weight at the end of a chain or cord.

There are many types available in shops and you should be able to find one that feels right for you. Or you can simply make your own. The weight should not be too heavy, nor too light. You can test it by asking the pendulum to show you what a "Yes" is and what a "No" is.

This is best done by resting your arm or elbow on a stable surface so as to minimise any interference from you or others that will prevent it from swinging freely and autonomously. It will guide itself, and you will find some pendulums respond better and more freely to your instruction than others. Choose from one of these when selecting one. You can also try shortening the length of its chain if the indication given appears to be too weak for you to read until you become familiar with the hidden energy mechanics of pendulum testing or dowsing.

If you do not get any response at all, either you are not clear enough with your intent or the pendulum is unable to read energy and respond to it. Crystal pendants are usually more reliable in providing feedback in this way than other substances.

I have also taken to attaching my pendulum to another longer horizontal crystal wand so that when I work with it, my fingers are not touching it, and it is suspended from the middle of the longer crystal.

You could use a piece of wood or anything else that creates a fulcrum effect if you wish.

Pendulums movements are generally:

- straight line - side to side or front and back
- circles - clockwise or counter-clockwise
- elliptical motion
- some pendulums bob up and down to indicate strong action, usually affirmative

PENDULUM ACTIONS

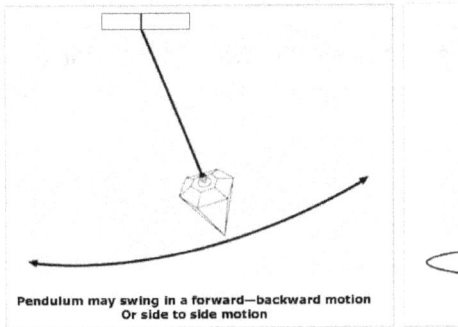

Pendulum may swing in a forward—backward motion
Or side to side motion

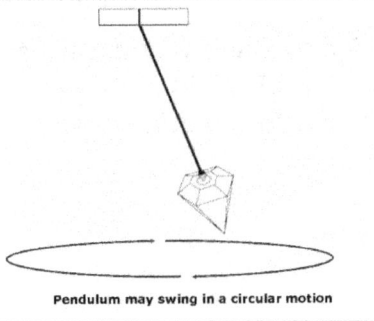

Pendulum may swing in a circular motion

When seeking an indication from the pendulum you must determine the direction your pendulum will take for Yes and for No.

Hold the pendulum in your stabilised hand. With the other hand - touch the point to steady its motion.

Keep your eyes on the point.

Now address the pendulum and say, **"Show me 'Yes'."** It will soon swing in one direction, which could be side to side, back and forth, or circles.

Now say, **"Show me 'No'."** It should swing in a different or opposite direction.

Be certain the pendulum is not being guided by the movement of your hand or fingers.

Once you have determined the pattern for Yes and No - you are ready to begin.

The faster the movement - the stronger the energies. Generally.

Testing the Crystal

Now you can hold or position the crystal pendulum over the crystal you are working with and ask it to "Show me what this crystal is doing". The pendulum will respond and indicate what is happening.

Refer to the chapter on *"Alignment Process for Crystals"* for complete instructions and to understand what the movement given means.

EVOLUTION

The intelligence of the energetic Being never failed to amaze me as the new Chakras revealed themselves. As we house more light and uptake more individual responsibility (and inner authority), we have evolved remarkable new anatomy.

Along with this evolutionary awareness, a new knowing has arrived for many of us, and so my previous use of crystals has had to change.

Even though they had been used for many years in my practice, I had come to a place where I did not require them in work as before for several years. It was as if I had somehow absorbed some of their capabilities and my energy systems seemed to have become so familiar with them to the point of being so in tune that I could consciously focus and use their amplifying frequency without needing to hold the actual physical crystal in order to access its particular frequency.

Then one day it seemed as if they had had changed and needed to work with me again in a different and more conscious way.

It was like a hand tapping me on the shoulder and saying 'Pay more attention!' as I listened to this call and began to use them again...

The fire experience heightened the understanding of current energetic shifts.

For over 20 years, Vibrational Healing tools and essences had been a natural part of my healing work. Now how I worked seemed to shift and change. And as I worked with the new human etheric energy systems, I realized my other vibrational tools had changed too.

Along with my knowledge that each Chakra does not simply resonate to one color alone, I now use my crystals with a new coding system along with my awareness of the new higher frequencies that are possible in our aura and Chakras. I call these codes The Cipher Codes.

Living in cities can hide some of these new hues and tints and prevent them from shining within and without, as the electromagnetic smog and pollution can lower frequencies to a paler and poorer version.

In these times it is becoming more important to reconnect back to nature, the land or the sea, purer energies, higher vibrations and natural remedies whenever and wherever possible to sustain us.

Before I share with you the new Cipher Codes and Alignment techniques, let us look at Crystals and their current understandings so we can build upon these.

Crystal Background

In order to align to the New Incoming Energies, let us consider some of the current knowledge of crystals, for we do not lose these – these form the basis for alignment after all.

How Crystals Grow

Generally, quartz crystals grow in a hexagonal (six sided) structure, with additional faces sloping towards a point at one end. A crystal with these features is itself called a point. Points may be totally clear, or may contain streaks, rainbows, water bubbles, or other inclusions.

They may also appear cloudy if they have grown in a place where it freezes in the winter. Optical clarity usually has little to do with the crystal's quality and ability to amplify subtle energies.

There are a variety of crystals that grow in various molecular formations – this gives them their energetic actions and properties. Clear quartz has a clear predictive charge because of its molecular structure and so it is used in watches for time-keeping accuracy.

Over time, specific minerals gather together from the atmosphere and environment, and together with heat and pressure from the earth depending on their geolocation within the earth, they concentrate and form the wonders of the many forms of gems we know today.

They are coloured by whatever minerals constitute them, giving us glorious purples, pinks, reds, yellows, greens, blues, and even deep dark blues and blacks.

CRYSTAL FORMATIONS

Crystals are formed out of an array of minerals, and are defined by its particular internal structure, like a lattice of orderly repeating atoms unique to each species of crystal. These formations can be based on the following shapes:

- triangle
- square
- trapezium
- rectangle
- rhomboid
- parallelogram and
- hexagon.

The atoms of a crystal are quite dynamic, though the crystal itself may give an outward serene appearance. Each crystal is actually a mass of molecules and atoms that are vibrating at certain frequencies – this is what gives it its energy and transforming and healing properties.

When you examine them closely, particularly the many varieties of quartz, you may find all sorts of markings, indentations or inclusions on or within them which assist in a variety of ways with their ultimate functions. These dictate what data they carry, what codes they hold.

How Crystals Work

Crystals have active molecules and atoms which allow them to act as a power source. They can store and amplify energy, as well as conduct and focus energy. They also possess piezoelectric properties, which means that they develop electric potential upon the application of mechanical stress or pressure.

They are also able to store light and discharge it, as you can see when you strike two crystals together in a darkened room. Though I do not recommend this with crystals you value or plan to work with... This inherent ability also shows that they fire up an energy that can be discharged. Crystals can also convert sunlight directly into electricity, as well as store information – a cut sliver of crystal can pick up a specified vibratory pattern, which can be 'frozen' and later 'unfrozen' to play back the original pattern or code. These silicon slivers or chips are found in many computers.

They may also cause an interference pattern when applied to muscles in a certain way which may prevent the extension of that particular muscle.

Energy and matter changes constantly. Our own bodies prove that, for underneath even seemingly unchanging exteriors, the body is always busy converting energy to what it needs. Life teaches us that nothing ever really stays the same – even though things that still exist yet never seem to change (historic monuments, stone castles etc) undergo processes of change. In fact matter can neither be created nor destroyed, only changed and Einstein proved that matter and energy are inextricably linked, energy can become matter and matter can become energy.

We are living in a time that indicates that science is at last catching up with the wisdom and the knowledge of the ancients as well as the study of Quantum physics with various new realisations, including the idea that thought precedes physicality.

Metaphysically put – Crystals are capable of receiving, containing, projecting, emanating, refracting and reflecting light, which is currently the highest form of energy known in our physical universe.

So crystals function according to their structure, composition, colour, shape, and programming.

With the new vortex energies, and the evolved crystal potential to bridge into different dimensions, the further understanding of crystals is also being enhanced. Aligning them with this new understanding brings further possibilities. The new Cipher Codes bring further clarity and power to those crystals who have been aligned with these new vortex energies.

CARING FOR CRYSTALS

There are many methods to use when it comes to caring for and handling crystals. We have listed some ways for you to try or consider. Sources of information are listed at the end of the book.

The first step of course, is to select or chose your crystal. Unless of course it has found its way to you as a gift from a caring friend.

Having selected or acquired your crystal, it may then be necessary to know how to use and care for it or them.

There are several distinct steps to follow to ensure that your crystal is not only suitable, but also ready to be used by you personally. It is important that you consider each step as part of the whole process of using your crystal. The distinct steps are:

1. Clean
2. Clear
3. Program
4. Maintain

Selecting Your Crystal

All crystals need to be treated with respect and love. If they are used as a tool, do so with humility and gratitude. Even though crystals will work 'on demand', I believe you may get more from it by honouring the consciousness or intelligence of each crystal with appreciation. In choosing a crystal, it is necessary to find one that vibrates in harmony with the self and with the specific purpose for which you are bringing it into your life. Like attracts like.

Each human and each crystal has its own vibration.

Suppose that in front of you is a tray of crystal quartz and others. Look at them... Feel them...

There are a number of ways to know which is right for you.

Instant rapport - is there one that you are instantly drawn to?

Strong energies - move your hand over the top and feel the energies from each and see which one you are drawn to.

Physical attraction - is there one that you really like the look of and must pick it up and feel it?

The Crystal chooses You - Is there a crystal that appears to 'wink' or 'glow' when you look at it, that appears to be trying to signal or speak to you? If so, this is probably a crystal you should pay attention to.

If you are not sure how to choose, then use this method following.

To select a crystal, first put yourself in a calm frame of mind. Hold the crystal in your hands with the point towards you and feel it physically. Be open to any feelings such as tingling, changes in temperature or other sensations. Then be aware of the crystal emotionally. Think of the purpose you want for it, such as: healing, intuition, dream work...and see if you feel attracted to this particular crystal. Be more concerned with how the crystal feels to you rather than how it looks. Allow the crystal to pick you by interacting with it in this way. And remember to go with your initial feeling.

Crystals That Never Need Cleaning

The crystals that are generally noted to not need cleaning are Kyanite, Citrine and Azeztulite. However, they may appreciate a moon bath occasionally. There are some other crystals that some may think do not need clearing or may never need it.

However, it is my opinion that **all** crystals benefit from some 'clearing' or loving attention to assist them in recharging their energies.

Crystals That Clean Other Crystals

Some crystals can be used to clean other crystals, which is particularly useful if you don't have the time between uses to do a full cleaning or the full moon is not imminent. These crystals are Amethyst, Carnelian and Clear Quartz.

Of course, these crystals will need to be cleaned regularly themselves, as they are not necessarily self cleaning.

Wearing Crystals

Crystals can often be worn for particular vibrational effects, and after checking for suitability regarding their abilities, and your compatibility with the crystal, check for appropriateness regarding position on the body.

Usually when worn around the neck, they can stimulate the thyroid and increase the efficiency of the immune system. They can assist with the respiratory system and sore throats. In the case of Black Tourmaline, they can assist with electro-magnetics. Crystal pendants or neck jewellery can be worn with adjustable or longer chains to work on the heart or solar plexus area. When the crystal is pointing down it is usually grounding, soothing and calming. They can also be used to give energy to all of the systems, depending on the shape of the crystal worn.

Particular care should be taken when wearing rings due to meridians running along the fingers. For instance, rubies can be of supreme support for motivation and protection, but can also bring up anger, passion or heightened awareness. And if you are of a nervous disposition, this may create even more nervousness or over stimulation. If placed on the middle or little fingers, which are connected with the heart and pericardium protecting the heart, ruby may over activate the meridians. So do a little research before investing in gem quality crystals.

And of course, always clean your crystal of any unwanted energies that they may have picked up through handling etc *before* you begin to wear them!

Using and Working with Crystals

Apart from the above suggestions about choosing a crystal, when deciding on one for healing work, if you are confident enough, you should use your own intuition, and you may also choose to self-test to support what feels the right choice. The more you learn and know about crystals, the application of them will be more effective when using these unique vibrational healers and helpers.

This book presents some of the possible uses of crystals. Correct use of crystals can make the difference between enhancement of one's energy field and the 'bringing down' of one's energy.

There are many uses for crystals, for the self, the home, and for assisting others.

Sometimes there is an initial reaction from working with a new crystal, as it starts clearing out of your energy fields vibrations that are not in harmony with the crystals vibration. If this occurs, observe, and maybe give yourself a rest for a day or so before wearing or using again. Always note any reactions that you experience. Sometimes one is not yet ready to work with a particular vibration. A safe way to test for a personal crystal is to carry one around for a little while, to gauge its effect. You may also choose to sleep with a smaller version of a crystal before purchasing a gem quality crystal to wear.

Warning

One thing I have noted – when wearing Clear Quartz jewellery, because of its actions, it will magnify everything and anything that is not of the Light, so if you are dealing with issues, it will bring them up "right in your face" so to speak – this can be a bit harsh sometimes. So gradually introduce it, and because of its magnification properties, wear it only on those occasions when you feel really good about yourself or about life – at first!

Intention - Centering One's Self

To use crystals effectively one needs to have a centred state of mind from which to work, and a clear intention of the purpose for the crystal.

As crystals amplify whatever energies are around them, whatever you are feeling may well be enhanced when crystals are close by. If you are feeling negative, choose a crystal that helps to clear the negativity, and to bring in more positive energy. [Sometimes using more than one crystal is indicated – depending on the issue.]

There is no need to make yourself neutral (unless you are working with clients), but rather to be aware of your own feelings so that your emotions can be managed, without allowing them to control, overwhelm or distract you from your intent. If, at any time you have difficulty in achieving or maintaining your centre, put your crystals aside and return to them later.

Crystal Cleaning

There are a variety of cleaning and clearing methods that you can use.

Cleaning vs Clearing Crystals

There is a difference between cleaning and clearing a crystal. Cleaning refers to the process of hygienically preparing the crystal, rendering it free from dirt, foreign matter, finger prints and grease, or dust etc. This is the very first step after selecting your crystal.

Crystals will also need periodic cleaning, as they can gather dust, and fluff. This can often help restore its original 'sparkle'. When you first get a crystal it will need cleansing and then clearing, as it will have picked up many energies on its way to you. It also needs cleaning when it is dirty, dusty or has body oil on it from handling. Just as you need a shower or bath on a regular basis, so does your crystals.

Many also like to bathe in the light of moon for periodic maintenance. This is sometimes referred to as having a 'moon' bath'.

There are several ways of doing this. Clear quartz crystals can be left in full sunlight for a day, also in full moonlight. Running water is good, fresh water, streams, rivers.

Visualisation of the crystal in a mountain stream or flooded with white light, is also a good way.

Your intent should be pure and clear, and when using water <u>never use hot or warm water</u>.

Please note though that sometimes in the cleaning of the crystal and depending on the method used, you may also achieve clearing it of negative energies.

Previous programs installed in your crystal will require the clearing process.

Crystals To Keep Dry

Special Note: Some stones that don't do well at all in Salt OR Fresh water are

- Azurite
- Calcite
- Carnelian
- Celestite
- Chrysocolla
- Fuschite
- Galena
- Gypsum
- Halite
- Hematite
- Kyanite
- Labradorite/Spectrolite
- Lepidolite
- Lodestone (Magnetite)
- Magnesite
- Mica
- Moldavite
- Opal
- Selenite
- Seraphanite
- Stichtite
- Turquoise
- Ulexite

and there are surely more. When you do use salt water for crystal cleaning, do so cautiously and don't leave your crystals in it longer than absolutely necessary.

Stone clusters and geodes are two types of stones that do not do well with water, as they may break apart and crumble.

1. CLEANING:

The following methods are generally suitable for cleansing most crystals – [first check for the exceptions as above]:

§ Flower Water:

You can also clear crystals and stones in flower water. Soak the stone or crystal in water with the petals of rose, honey suckle, orange blossoms, jasmine or others for 24 hours. Again, the same cautions apply regarding stones that don't do well in water.

§ Wiping:

Wipe over with damp cloth dipped in flower water, or Serapis Bey (an AuraSoma product) essence or solution.

§ Air:

Use the breathe to **blow off** dust, or gentle cold hairdryer air stream to loosen dust etc. toothbrush can reach into crevices.

§ Salt Water:

Use With <u>CARE</u>. While this is a popular way to cleanse crystals, I recommend using salt water very carefully. You need to know about your crystals to be sure that they are not porous or soft, so they won't be damaged by water. Salt water can get into the structure of some crystals and stones and cause them to break or crumble.

For those hardy crystals, this is an excellent way to clean and clear them. Sea water is also an excellent cleansing and rejuvenating method. I have taken mine for a sea bathe and also rested them on the sand so that they have gained some sun, some earthing and some water energies.

§ **Tap Water**:

COOL Tap Water: For a quick cleansing, you can run your stones under cool tap water. Hot or warm water is a no-no, because it can fracture some crystals and stones.

Again, as with salt water, be sure that your crystals are not porous or soft, before putting them under the tap. The stones mentioned as not doing well with salt water may also not do well with tap water. Also, with water restrictions, please do conserve water and preferably use another method. However, fresh running spring water is extremely effective due to the ions in the water.

2. CLEARING

Clearing is the process of changing negative emotions to positive emotions. Anyone who holds a crystal and is having bad feelings, negative emotions, may imprint those emotions into the crystal. It is also a way to clear old programs.

§ **Invocation**: A very good and effective method for clearing a crystal is to use Invocation. Here is one that was passed on to me - hold or touch your crystal with your hand. Repeat the following light invocation or phrase it in terms that work for you and state three times as follows;

"I invoke the Light of the Pure God-ness / Divine within. I am a clear and perfect channel. Divine Light is my guide."

By the time, you have completed the third repetition; the attached negative emotion will be gone.

§ **Breathe and Intent:** Personally, I mostly use this following technique – I Hold fast this statement in my mind or verbally state it out loud and clearly:

"As I connect with my True Divine Source, I request that this Crystal is purified from all negative energies, which are now sent for appropriate spiritual transformation. This Crystal is now cleaned and cleared and recharged with light and pure energy.

So be it, so be it, so be it."

Taking a breath, I blow out through my mouth quickly like blowing out a candle in an action that is intended to set and seal the instruction. I may need a couple more breathes to complete the process (if it is particular nasty energy that is being cleared), but the first breathe I blow out, I blow it into the crystal, as though I am blowing away any cobwebs it has absorbed within. So my intention is to use my breath to clear the crystal as well as to set my intention clearly with it. Any other breathes I feel I need to take are simply the result of clearing and processing anything that is other than the truth of my statement that exists within the crystal or the space that I am in.

Using the alignment technique I describe at the end of the book, you can pendulum or test for its energy reading before and after this process.

§ **Energy**: Charging your chosen crystal using healing energy such as Ki-force, Reiki, Prana or other Universal Healing Energy is another method for clearing and cleansing crystals. Channel the chosen universal life force energy to heal the crystal of negativity and unwanted energies, using intent and focusing your intent through the finger-tips holding the crystal, or through the palm chakra in the hand. As you use the appropriate energy, set your intent to clear and heal the stone of any negativity or unwanted energies.

§ **Stone Clearing**: Some stones will clear the negative or unwanted energies from other stones. I know of quartz crystal clusters and Selenite. Place the stone to be cleared on a cluster of quartz or a piece of Selenite, and leave for 24-48 hours.

§ **Sunlight or Moonlight**: The rays of the sun and moon are very clearing and cleansing. Placing your stones outside where they can soak up the sunlight or moonlight for a day/night to a week is very beneficial. Do be careful though, as some the colours of some stones may fade in the sun. A few of the stones that will fade in the sun are Amethyst, Celestite, Opal, and Turquoise. If you have any doubts at all, be sure to use only moonlight cleansing.

§ **Lay on Earth** - Some crystals thrive on being placed on earth or soil regularly. If you don't have much garden, you can use a pot plant, and the plants love the vibrational energy too. Really energetically dirty crystals may need a few days, or even a couple of weeks to totally clean off, and if they are an Amethyst or similar, avoid placing in sunlight, as they will fade in colour.

§ **Earth Burial**: Burying crystals and stones is very cleansing and healing to them. You can bury them in the Earth for 3 days to a week, either in your yard or in a flowerpot. Be sure that if you bury your crystals in the yard that you mark the spot. You don't want to have to dig up half the yard to find your stones again. Clean Sand can also be used.

§ **Smudging**: Smudging is one of my favourite methods of clearing crystals and stones of unwanted energy. It's also a much quicker way to clear crystals than any of the above methods. To smudge them, pass you stone several times through the smoke of burning cedar, sage, sweetgrass, or incense. Commercial incenses with perfumy smells may not clear as fully or as quickly as sage or a more basic incense like Nag Champa.

§ **Sea Salt**: Some Crystals and jewellery can be placed in coarse sea salt for up to 24 hours to clear them. [Make sure that they are not adversely affected by salt first.] They can also be stored in sea salt to keep them from picking up energies from their surroundings.

§ **Serapis Bey** essence or solution is an excellent method. This is an AuraSoma essence product, which purifies through the use of clarified and concentrated herbs, vibrational essences and color.

Whichever method you choose, the exact length of time needed for clearing varies according to personal taste and the state of the crystal. Always cleanse after it has been used in any sort of healing and when you want to re-program it.

3. PROGRAMMING CRYSTALS

In metaphysical terms, programming a crystal is to store an energy pattern in a crystal. Crystals can receive and hold thought forms. When this is done consciously, it is called programming. The energy pattern programmed into the crystal can be any thought, colour, emotion, sound, or any other vibration. The vibrational pattern is stored in the crystal until it is purposefully cleared out. The programming of a crystal in relatively simple terms is the process of consciously creating a vibration or set of vibrations in a crystal and storing them in the crystal for later and/or continuing effect. There is a school of thought that the only crystal that can be programmed is quartz. I personally do not necessarily think that this is so.

Always first make sure your crystal is cleansed and cleared of any other negative emotions, thoughtforms or unsupportive programs. Here are some ideas to work with...

"This crystal is now 100% free from any previous programs"

"This crystal is now 100% clear of the programs of others and ready to work with me"

I don't believe there is only one way to do it, but rather many, and you should choose the one(s) that suit you best.

Even though crystals are not human, in that they do not have emotions of their own, they are willing to work with us in whatever way they can, using their natural pre-set power and ability.

Many crystals can give you a guide as to what they can be used for when you take the time to observe them closely and when you apply some knowledge of the chakras or the language of color. And when you discover its Crystal Cipher Code, you can really work with it effectively...

Always remember to separate your energies from the crystal after programming in order for it to perform its tasks impeccably and without interference – unless it is for your own personal use alone.

Here are some programming suggestions.

No 1 – The Breathe and 'Intention'

A simple method of programming is as follows: After first cleaning and clearing your crystal from any earlier programs, sit in a quiet place and still your mind. Let your crystal feel like a friend, like someone willing to work with you and for you. Feel comfortable and familiar with it. Think clearly about your intended purpose and what thought you want the crystal to hold. Always be clear how you want the crystal to work with you or what you wish for it to do.

Take a deep breath, and whilst holding the crystal in your left hand, blow your intention onto / into the crystal. This is a very powerful way to program the crystal. You can program a crystal to help you do most things. Try and use different crystals for separate programs or uses.

No 2 – Visualisation

This programming technique uses Visualisation and Instruction with Imagination and Feeling

Below is a suggestion for a complete process:

1. Formulate a precise phrase which accurately describes the nature of the programming [i.e. angelic/otherworldly communication, harmony, support, balance, love, special healing or protection for someone, etc] … "I request that

2. Hold the crystal in the left hand [if left-handed, hold the crystal in the right hand], relax for several minutes, initiate circular breathing, and centre the consciousness. Consciously align the personal conscious awareness with the Higher Self and/or other predefined appropriate otherworldly beings. Ask for guidance, protection, and assistance in the programming process. Open the centre of consciousness and allow receptivity to flow through the inner being.

3. Repeat the formulated phrase several times (up to 20-30 if necessary) in succession while visualising and/or feeling the desired effect of the program. [Be open to higher assistance during this process]. As the phrase is repeated, an energy field will build and culminate in the energy pattern necessary to represent the desired program. This will begin to imprint itself upon your crystal.

4. [This next action may not always be absolutely necessary in my opinion as connection can be made without, and should be used only when you will be working solely with the crystal yourself and for your own use alone. If being used for someone else or for healing of others, first check to see if this step is appropriate for you and your particular crystal.] While maintaining full awareness of the energy field, bring total awareness and consciousness to the area of heart chakra. Place the crystal in front of the area of the heart chakra and allow the self to feel the connection with it.

5. Direct the energy field into the crystal for 30-60 seconds and allow the program to be transferred to within the crystal. Intuitive recognition will signal when the transmittal is complete.

6. Detach consciousness from the crystal and allow its energies to act. With any crystal being used for others, ensure that at the end of the process that you *separate*

your energies from the crystal so that it can work unhindered.

No 3 – Breathe and Both Hands

1. Clean and clear the crystal that is to be programmed.

2. Hold the crystal in your both of your hands while gazing into it.

3. Centre yourself and clear your mind. Concentrate on that with which you intend to program the crystal.

4. As you retain your concentration, inhale and forcefully exhale through your mouth. It is as if you are blowing your intention into the crystal.

5. Continue this process until you feel satisfied that you have completely filled the crystal with your intention

The desired vibration is now stored in the crystal until you clear it out of the crystal. Some methods feel that a program is 'locked' into a crystal more effectively when steps one through five are done in <u>front of</u> a flame. Then when you are through programming the crystal, you pass it right to left through the flame. (*Take care when using fire or flame.*) This seals in the intended programming. When the programming is done, clear yourself, and the environment around you. When you want the program to be out of the crystal, just clear the crystal

Having programmed your crystal, it can them be carried with you, to be held, looked at, or thought of during the event for which you have prepared. The crystal retains the programmed thought form and will emanate that vision back to you, acting as an assistant and friend.

No 4 - Third Eye Program

First, determine the purpose of the program.

Then imagine what the end result would look like when the program is fully completed – how it would be when the program worked.

Next place the crystal against your brow Chakra or Third Eye. Don't worry too much about which direction the crystal is pointing as it does not matter. With your eyes closed focus upon and go inside your crystal.

Again, imagine your original thoughts, and picture the actions and the end result happening inside your crystal.

Build up the feelings and the senses associated with the desired outcome. Let the crystal interpret the program required, as it will pick up the vibrations you are emitting and will capture them in thought and wave-form as a program. Create it with as many of your senses as you can. See it, smell it, touch it, hear it, taste it, make it real.

When it feels real, come back out of your crystal, thanking it for its help and assistance, and separate your emotionality from it – feel the assurance that the crystal will be working for you toward this desired effect. Separate yourself from the crystal in gratitude. Then open your eyes.

No 5 - For Self Use

To program, first take the time to be grounded, uninterrupted and pure of heart. Be aware that what you think and feel will be captured and held by the crystal - so intend that only positive energies should be put into the stone/s. Generally you need to program them one at a time.

If you are right handed, hold the stone in your left hand. That is your receptive hand and you want to bring the intent into the stone. If you are left-handed, the reverse is true so hold the stone in your right hand.

You also need to know the general meanings of a stone to program it effectively. (There are many books to get an idea and some information on some of the most commonly used crystals in this book.)

Get into a calm meditative state, in thought language or audibly, (it's your preference) tell the stone what you want help with. Be clear when talking to it. Ask clearly, and confidently, do not plead. Be specific, tell the stone what you need and want.

Always thank the Earth and the Crystal Devas for assistance and the crystal.

No 6 – For Use with Others

This is one way to program a crystal so that you or someone else can benefit later from the energy pattern programmed into it.

Needed to Program Your Crystal:

· Crystal

· Clear Intent - Know what you want to program the crystal to do.

· Focused Action - This method is on focused action.

Step One – After cleaning and clearing with whatever method you prefer, sit down with your crystal at your personal altar or in a place that you're not likely to be disturbed while you are programming your crystal. .

Step Two - Hold the crystal in your dominant hand (right hand if right handed) and clear your mind of unrelated thoughts. Start to focus on your intention for the programming of your crystal.

Step Three - Focus on your intention for your crystal by saying descriptive words aloud. For instance, if you want to program your crystal to bring peace of mind, start repeating the words "peace of mind" over and over again.

(If others are nearby, then a whisper is fine if a normal tone of voice would attract distracting attention.)

Step Four - Repeat your intent verbally into your non-dominant hand, then place that hand over your crystal to push the vibrations into the crystal.

Step Five - Continue holding the crystal and repeating your intention until it feels as though the vibrations have sunk into the crystal fully. If necessary, repeat step four.

Once your intuition tells you or you have a sense that the crystal has accepted the vibrations, open your hands and thank the crystal. The crystal is now programmed.

This method can also be used with tumbled stones, spheres, polished crystals, and natural chunks of minerals, as well as natural crystals.

To retrieve and use the programming, simply rub the crystal while asking (silently or out loud) for its programming to be released.

4. MAINTENANCE

Clean Regularly!

On a physical level, handling crystals can grub them up somewhat with natural skin oils, and they can also gather dust. Cleanse appropriately, taking care that you use water cleaning only on crystals that can handle it.

On an energetic level, Crystals often need to be charged up, somewhat like a car battery. It is possible that they have not only absorbed a lot of toxic energies and been busy clearing and supporting, but they can become overwhelmed with dead energy and simply stop working. This is why regular attention can be required for those you use a lot or that are in a prominent position in your home or office.

The way to do this is very similar to cleansing.

Again you can use nature and leave in the sun, under the moon, any holy place, by stream or river. Leave as long as you feel is right. Don't leave them in drawers or dark places, wherever possible they like to be out in the open to work to their full potential.

Crystals accumulate, hold steady and emit energy charges. Generally speaking, the larger a crystals physical mass, the greater it's clarity, the fewer the internal or surface fractures it has, the larger its overall energy capacity will be.

The exceptions are the Rainbows seen within clear quartz crystals, as these refractions of light are signs of joy and happiness, and can help with depression, and the Self-Healed.

Other exceptions to this would include crystals that have been worked with extensively by an experienced individual, those crystals which have been 'en-lightened' by spiritual intervention and those that are members of matched sets of grid work crystals. A crystal's given charge is the feel you get from it as it radiates.

The different 'moods' and dynamics of each variety of crystal that can be used are as perfect and quiet as a rose flower or as mighty and as loud as a storm.

Using a pendulum and watching its motion, speed and pattern can give you an indication of its effectiveness and nature.

For Healers

A quality geode of Amethyst cut in 2 provides a wonderful recluse for well used crystals. Large Amethyst clusters and geodes are excellent for both cleansing and charging purposes. It can handle a constant demand providing this cluster is, itself, cared for.

Exposure to environmental and natural sources will create a response in a crystal. Put your moonstone out in a blue moon, or your diamond to the sun. The rhythms of nature and the rising tide can each be helpful, they can all inspire.

You may also leave a crystal in an energy vortex, a sacred place or those areas filled with positive vibes. The abundance of freshness can be captured from a waterfall or the beauty of a field of daffodils.

Just like the recall of a fond moment in time, a crystal can replay any vibration you wish to inlay or 'program' it with.

Charging Crystals

From time to time, crystals appreciate a refresh, a recharge, particularly when they have been working with clearing and energising tasks. Leaving them out during a full moon can be a great way to enhance and recharge them again, they really seem to like this energy and can sparkle even more after this.

Protect those that don't appreciate too much water from the rain, whilst water resilient crystals enjoy lying out on the grass and connecting with earth energies as well as moon energies during their recharge.

Charging a stone with your own energetic intent is also a skill you can learn.

In the same way one clears a crystal with intent and breath, you can charge a stone with any concept or feel that you can hold focused in your mind.

Crystals right now also require a new alignment, a new reordering of their frequencies, a new link in with humanity, planetary, global and cosmic energies.

Crystal Healing

Over the years, I have used a variety of crystals, often intuitively, and find I am always learning something new. Consequently I sometimes forget an old use, so now I choose to no longer get hung up on trying to remember everything. Crystals are always willing to assist, and now they are ready for a new alignment with the energies of this current age in order to expand their abilities even further.

Trauma or Shock

When someone has had etheric, emotional or spiritual shock of any kind, it can weaken the fabric or substance of their etheric fields and auric envelopes. What their energy systems will require (generally) initially, is for a strengthening of these energy bodies.

Crystals are a very powerful vibrational remedy, and care must be taken with particularly sensitive or energetically and aurically damaged people.

Points in particular are like lasers, and can create damage when used incorrectly or thoughtlessly, as they can penetrate or cut the etheric. This is good for clearing and cutting out negative energy, but if this is entangled with the etheric webbing or fabric, then one just may create more damage.

So please take extra care in the type and shape of crystal you use, particularly with those who have been through a rough traumatic time, or who have weakened auras through psychic attacks, pathological energies or splintered auric bodies. And especially avoid using crystals with points around damaged or vulnerable auras and chakras.

With trauma of any kind, using the *rounded* stone or pebble of a crystal can give them a gentle flow of energy rather than a forceful energy which can feel too overwhelming for some. Sometimes using stones in the shape of a heart or flat pancake like circular shape can be very comforting. The same energy is activated, but is delivered in a more easily assimilated form.

It may also be wise to check the suitability of the potential actions of the chosen crystal so that when someone is going through a rough time, the crystal qualities support them, rather than forcefully breaking down internal or energetic blockages which may further energetically push them into more trauma or crisis.

You will need to be discerning when assessing which priority to work with first – supporting or clearing, stabilizing or changing etc… and you may find you can possibly do some of both at different times during the session.

Generally, I start with Citrine to help stabilize and protect generally and gently. I often use rutilated quartz pebbles, a powerful healer that works on re-knitting the nadis in the chakras, and repairing the entire auric fields.

Rutilated quartz also clears as it heals. I find that the aura more easily stabilizes and this allows for continual integration of all of the auric bodies during a balance so that less work needs to be performed.

Normal Sessions

Besides the Citrine as already mentioned, I might also add further crystals to create stability of the energies whilst working for change. Once the trauma has been dealt with and the energy fields stabilised and strengthened, I can introduce more powerful transformation crystals into later sessions.

If the client is just in need of general energetic support, I generally place smoky quartz near the base chakra on the floor under the massage table, and quartz points under the upper part of the body, roughly near the heart and solar plexus. These form a basic grid formation that allows for deeper access to, and a good stabilizing basis to keep the client present and grounded whilst accessing deeper levels and other dimensions.

Crystal Grids can be used to access and clear specific Chakras or meridian systems. There are many types of grids, and if you are using kinesiology, you can test up for the appropriate ones to use for each individual client at each individual session. Always bear in mind though, not only what the most effective crystals are for the session, but also the best and most comforting crystal energies for the client at that particular time. Each client and each situation is individual; nevertheless, you may find yourself using particular grids regularly.

It helps to have some idea of why you are choosing a particular stone or gem when you work with crystals. Knowing something about the type of crystal can certainly and obviously assist, but if you can muscle-test or pendulum test, this can be both helpful and illuminating.

Quartz Power

Quartz comes in so many shapes and sizes, as well as colours.

Here we look initially at the basic qualities of this stone as well as how they can be enhanced when they posses various formations or distinguishing features.

Then we look at their various distinguishing features.

Quartz possesses both piezoelectrical and pyroelectrical qualities.

Piezoelectricity: *When quartz crystals are subjected to mechanical pressure, they produce a consistent and measureable electrical voltage. When an electrical current is applied to a crystal, it will induce mechanical movement. The tips of phonograph needles as used in record players can transduce mechanical vibrations from the patterns in the grooves into electrical oscillation, which can then be translated by the electronics in the record player into music and words.*

Pyroelectricity *is the ability of certain mineral crystals to generate an electrical potential when they are heated or cooled. As a result of this change in temperature, positive and negative charges move to the opposite ends of the crystal through migration as the material becomes polarized. In this way an electrical potential is established.*

QUARTZ - Rock Crystal

Rock Lore and Tidbits: Quartz is the most common mineral on the planet. It is a component of a huge variety of rock types, and comes in an extensive range of colours and varieties. Chalcedony is a crypto-crystalline variety of quartz and includes the agate and jasper families. Many colours of quartz or formations have their own names, such as Amethyst for purple quartz. The word quartz is thought to come from the German word "quartz", but the origin of that word is not known. The word crystal, however, comes from the Greek word "krystallos" which means ice. Ancient Japanese believed quartz formed from the breath of a white dragon, and regarded it as representing perfection. Australian Aborigines used quartz in rain rituals. Crystal skulls were reportedly made by Atlanteans and are believed by some to be living entities. Clear quartz formed into spheres have been used as crystal balls to predict the future at least since the Middle Ages.

Metaphysical and Healing Properties

Keywords: Power, Clarity

Quartz is a power stone. It has been called the "Universal Crystal", and is the most recognised type of crystal. It's what many people envision when they think of crystals, even though there are many types of crystals. Quartz can be icy clear or have inclusions, veils, bubbles, etc. Visual clarity normally isn't important to a quartz crystal's energetic quality and ability to amplify subtle energies.

Quartz enhances energy by absorbing, storing, amplifying, balancing, focusing and transmitting. It channels universal energy. Quartz also enhances thoughts, as they are a form of energy. Because it directs and amplifies energy, it is extremely beneficial for manifesting, healing, meditation, and channeling. It is also beneficial for storing and retrieving information of all types, as information is a form of energy pattern also. This makes them particularly good for programming. Due to its ability to balance, quartz is excellent for harmonising and balancing one's environment. Quartz is also good for energising other crystals.

Quartz is a stone of clarity which dispels negativity and clears away negative energy. It can be used to purify and clarify on the spiritual, mental, and physical planes. Quartz enhances spiritual growth, spirituality and wisdom. Because it clarifies though processes and emotions it increases inspiration and creativity. It can also help particularly with concentration, studying, and retaining what one learns. Quartz is also a stone of harmony because it balances energies, and is even helpful in romantic relationships.

Psychically, quartz is a powerful stone. It is often used for protection because it is said that it can counter black magic and protect from negative energy. Quartz is very useful on the third eye chakra for clarity of psychic vision, and can be used to communicate with spirits and other worlds. Quartz is a stone that can access ancient wisdom and bring it into the present. It is a very good stone for astral travel, manifestation, scrying, channeling, dream recall and dream work.

Quartz is a Master Healer stone. It is an excellent all-purpose healer. It amplifies healing energy and is used to perform diagnostic healing. It has been used historically to detect food poison. It is said to draw out pain. Quartz fortifies and strengthens all systems of the body. Quartz is reputed to be particularly effective for chronic fatigue, arthritis, bone injuries, depression, fibromyalgia, and intestinal troubles. It also improves mental and physical energy, stamina, and physical strength.

Quartz is further enhanced when it is combined with certain types of distinguishing features. These usually come in the form of certain kinds of sides or 'faces' which help to focus the energy of the crystal. Varying numbers of sides provide varying properties and functions which can be applied for different intentions and purposes.

The above qualities apply to all Quartz crystals, and they can be further enhanced by various structural characteristics which add to their properties.

CHANNELING CRYSTAL – 7 sides

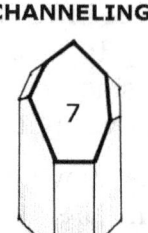

Have seven edges surrounding the largest sloping face. These crystals are especially useful for obtaining information from deep within yourself or from sources that are outside your normal realm. They can help you draw on the knowledge and information that is provided by the universe, and can aid you in getting help from a higher source. A channeling crystal can be used anytime you are seeking answers or help from outside of yourself. You must 'listen' very carefully when using this crystal and realise that answers can come from many sources.

Communication with Guide: A channeling crystal is a line of communication with sources outside yourself. Generally, the main source is your guide. A guide is a non-physical entity whose primary job is to look after you. Every human being has a guide. Guides are sometimes called other things, such as conscience, or angels, but they are always with us. We must learn to listen to what they have to say. Your guide will never tell you what to do, or interfere in other ways with what you want to do, but your guide is there to help you find answers foe yourself. And you can use your channeling crystal to let your guide be your conscience.

A channeling crystal can only be used by the person holding it. In other words, you can't send the energy to someone else in order to let him receive the information directly. However, since guides communicate readily with each other, you can become good at getting information to people by asking your guide to give you the needed information for someone else, and then relaying it to the person. This is how you channel information for others. Channeling crystals amplify the quiet inner voice of your guide, and can be a big help in learning how to channel information, both for yourself and for others.

EXERCISE: sit quietly holding the channeling crystal in your hand and focus on or consider the problem or area that you need help with. 'Listen' carefully but remember that the answer might not come immediately. Often, in the beginning, you may find that you wake up some morning and seem to 'Know' what to do. When you are working on a problem, keep the channeling crystal with you as much as possible and keep it close at night. Sometimes that is the only time the answers can come clearly when you are just starting to open your eyes.

CRYSTALS WITH BABIES

Crystals that are tiny crystals growing inside a larger crystal are called "babies". These are very good for people who have had traumatic childhoods, physically or mentally. They are helpful for people who are blocking painful memories. They help bring the cause of pain to the surface and allow the person to successfully deal with it, while shielding that person from the pain those memories can cause. These crystals work well for people who are working through current family problems.

Work slowly with this type of crystal so things can be cleared at your own pace. You may not feel inclined to work with it at all in the beginning. Don't force yourself. When you feel ready, you will find yourself drawn to that particular crystal. You may have this crystal for years before you are ready to use it.

Also, sometimes crystals come to you so that they can go to someone else. For example, someone might receive a crystal with babies, have it for some time and not be drawn to it at all. Suddenly they will have an urge to pass it on to someone else.

You can use this crystal in meditation or just keep it close to you. Just be prepared to deal with whatever comes up. Try to have some sort of support around you if you are going to work with this crystal.

DOUBLE TERMINATED CRYSTALS ↕

Are crystals that have points on both ends, allowing energy to flow readily in both directions. Double terminated crystals strengthen energy flow, and are especially useful when you need to share or exchange energy between you and another person. They are useful when you are working to help other people, for example in massage counselling, where energy needs to flow in both directions. In these situations, energy flows towards you when you tune in to a person to find out what the person needs, and energy flows from you when you give the person the needed healing energy. Double terminated crystals are very important to people doing healing work for themselves or others. They also teach sharing through energy exchange.

EXERCISE: If you are feeling out of balance with the world, sit quietly and hold the double terminated crystal in your right hand. Visualise white light flowing into the first point, through the crystal and out the other point directly into your body.

If you have children, try using this crystal to send positive energy to the child when the child is upset or angry. It can have a very calming effect on the both of you.

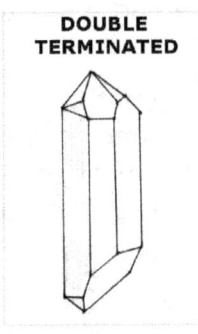

DOUBLE TERMINATED

ELESTIALS QUARTZ CRYSTALS

Elestial crystals are defined as those crystals which are identified by the natural terminations over the body and faces, resembling a skeletal structure. They tend to have double terminations like a large diamond-like shape.

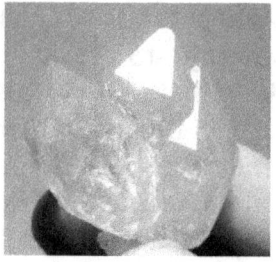

There can be triangular protrusions or etchings that seem to sit on the surface, and which look like lots of little points overlapping each other.

They may come in a variety of colours including clear, Amethyst, Citrine and even orange. Some can be a smoky colour, generally smoky Citrine or smoky quartz. These are extremely powerful crystals and are believed to have been brought into this reality, at this time, to assist in the mass cleansing, healing, and reawakening that is currently occurring on this plane of existence.

Elestials are also great comforters to those who are in the dying process and they assist to release the fear of leaving the physical body in order to identify the mortality of the soul.

Elestials may also contain rainbows. Mostly they look as though they have double and multi-terminated crystals all melded into one.

Some may have clear edges that lead into mists or 'fog'. They can be very complex and as with most elestials and a lot of other crystals, it can appear that every time you look into it, there is always something different to see!

Besides the rainbows, they may contain some mica inclusions which can also further enhance the clear elestials. Some can possess a top or major side that is almost an icy window to the inclusions and minerals found within.

Elestial quartz crystals are attuned to the vibration of the higher spiritual realms and they can assist you to make a stronger connection to these realms. They can continuously receive spiritual vibrations, which when aligned correctly can regulate and attune to the energy close by.

This then allows you to receive an infusion of the love and light from the higher realms without it impacting you in a way that may be uncomfortable. They provide a stronger connection to spirit and to the angelic realms.

FADEN CRYSTAL

The Faden has a flat look to it, and is usually formed from a TABULAR (Flat) Crystal however it tends toward six sides, and has a distinct line of white-cloudy thread of gas going through it.

A Master Healer, it helps heal the connection between soul and body, strengthens the Soul and being and aids internal communication providing healing and clarity.

ISIS CRYSTALS – 5 sides

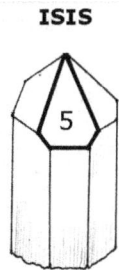

The Isis crystal has five edges surrounding the largest sloping face. These crystals strongly amplify the feminine energy. They can help you get in touch with the 'female' or unselfish side of yourself, no matter whether you are a man or women. These crystals are useful in balancing your male-female energy if the female energy is suppressed, or if you need a greater balance of female energy for any reason. Isis crystals put you in touch with the power of the goddess.

For men, the Isis crystal will help you become more in tune with your feminine side and to become more aware of the aspects of women that you may find more troubling.

For women, the Isis crystal will help you regain some of the power and energy that society has taken from you. Teaches that feminine is not weak. Anyone doing healing work with another person needs Isis energy to be effective.

The Isis crystal should be carried or held when dealing with issues that are emotional and difficult.

EXERCISE: Isis crystals can be used to project nurturing energy toward another person (permission!). To do this, sit quietly with the Isis crystal in your hand with the point directed away from you. Visualise the person that you wish to help and visualise white light going from the point of the crystal and surrounding the person. (Then disconnect).

To nurture yourself, sit with the Isis crystal in your hand with the point directed towards you. Visualise a white light going from the point of the crystal and surrounding you. After doing this you should feel strong and cared for.

GROUNDING CRYSTALS – 8 sides

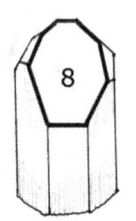

GROUNDING

Have eight edges surrounding the largest sloping face. They are quite rare and not always easily available. Grounding is the ability to deal with practical matters in a realistic way. For example, in dealing with the question 'how am I going to make a living', a grounded person will consider his skills and decide how best to use those skills to make a living. An ungrounded or 'spacey' person does not like to deal with the practical or realistic aspects of life.

Grounding crystals help you deal with practical matters in a realistic way. They connect you with the earth and keep your energies from being scattered. They help you think clearly and express yourself clearly.

When used in meditation they help you from a strong connection with higher knowledge, but keep you grounded so that you can apply that information in practical terms. When using a grounding crystal to work through a personal problem, remember that it will require you to look at the truth of the situation and compel you to deal with the truth.

It is sometimes difficult to recognise times when you need this crystal because not being grounded can be a way of life for some people.

These days, it is common to be a little spacey because of things going on in our world. When you are having trouble concentrating, feeling reluctance to tackle a task that needs doing, or find yourself running in circles but accomplishing nothing, you need a grounding crystal.

EXERCISE: Sit quietly holding the crystal. Visualise yourself firmly rooted to the earth. Breathe deeply and visualise the roots going deeper into the earth. Continue this exercise until you feel calm and peaceful. When you are having a 'spacey' time be sure to keep your grounding crystal close to you. Some people may need to keep it with them most of the time.

You can sometimes help another person become more grounded by sitting quietly, holding your grounding crystal, and visualising that person being firmly rooted to the earth. [Release energy ties at the end of the session.]

LEMURIAN QUARTZ CRYSTALS

Rainbows can often be viewed in some Lemurian crystals. The rainbows lend extra healing power to the crystal, speaking of color and beauty even where there has been a schism or inner "tear".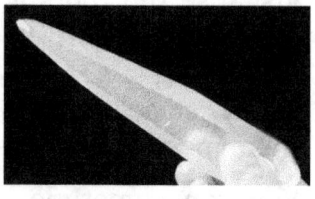
They often appear to be ice-clear towards the top point becoming denser or more opaque toward the bottom. Sometimes there can be linear or triangular etchings on the sides or "faces".

Lemurian crystals often come into a wand type shape, having a more narrow point at one of the ends. They usually have striations or appear "rough" with some of their markings, but inevitably they feel somehow lighter and finer than normal quartz wands. They may appear to be clear and white with striations, or can have a goldish hue to them.

There is a delicacy about them that differentiates them from normal quartz. They are a delight to work with as very powerful and effective healers, clearers and repairers. Take great care when using these crystals, as they are like lasers and must be used wisely.

Lemurian Crystals are sometimes referred to as Lemurian Seed Crystals which are classified as unity consciousness crystals because they help us reconnect to mother earth and universal love. The lore behind Lemurian Seed Crystals is that they were planted in mother earth by the ancient people of Lemuria many moons ago in order to "seed" future generations with their hidden information. All Lemurian crystals are energetically connected to each other. It is thought that each crystal contains unlocked mysteries to our ancient wisdom that can be accessed through the horizontal markings on the sides of the crystal.

QUARTZ CLUSTERS

These represent community and are very powerful at clearing any negative energy from the room. Just set one out somewhere and allow it to work to clear the environment.

CLUSTER

AMETHYST/SMOKEY CLUSTERS

These are powerful in keeping the spirit centred because they carry a special kind of energy that works toward assisting to keep all the energy centers within the body aligned, balanced, and in harmony with each other. They can also be quite helpful in cleansing an area or space, though if there has been a lot of people traffic, they will require regular maintenance.

RAINBOW CRYSTALS

Crystals that contain what looks like a rainbow reflected from within the crystal are referred to as Rainbow Crystals.

The rainbow is a colourful refraction of lights showing as an inner prism that can be present in almost any crystal, though it is more easily seen in transparent or mostly clear types of crystal.

Usually they are best viewed in sunlight. These crystals are especially good as meditation crystals for working deep within the subconscious. They work particularly well to lighten the mood for people experiencing sadness, grief or depression. Just holding a rainbow crystal can lighten your mood. Rainbow crystals are also very good at drawing negativity by letting it sit in the sunshine for a while.

EXERCISE: Rainbow crystals bring joy into your life. If you are sad or depressed sit and meditate on the rainbow. It can help lighten your mood. If working with another, let him/her hold the crystal if he/she is with you. If he is not with you, hold the rainbow and visualise white light leaving the rainbow and going to him.

RECORD KEEPERS ▲

Some crystals have tiny triangles on their faces, which may have been pre-programmed, or may be ready for your programs. When you rub the triangles or some of the sides or 'faces' of a crystal, it can deliver and activate its programs to you.

Crystals with these triangles are called Record Keepers for this reason. These pyramid shapes can be either indentations or similarly shaped elevations that appear to be etched on one of the sloping faces. They are generally fairly rare, and often the triangle or pyramid will not be noticed until the crystal comes into the hands of the person it was meant to work with. Sometimes the pyramid can disappear and sometimes more pyramids show up. Each of these crystals has its own special lesson to teach, sometimes with information and sometimes with a lesson the person most needs to learn.

Record keepers differ from window crystals in that window crystals help you look inside yourself to let you see various things you need to learn, while record keepers deal with a specific lesson that you need to learn. A record keeper may pass from your hands very quickly once the lesson is learned.

Carry your record keeper or put it close to your bed so that it can work with you. It can also be used for meditation.

Some crystals have several special characteristics, i.e. an Isis with a record. In this case there may be a specific lesson to learn that deals with the feminine side of your energy. If you have an Isis with a window it may mean that you need to look inside to find the areas in your feminine side that are causing you problems.

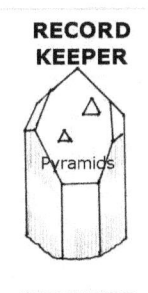

RECORD KEEPER

PYRAMIDS

SELF-HEALED and PHANTOM CRYSTALS

A self-healed crystal is one that has been broken off and damaged quite badly, but then begins to grow again or seal over the jagged part.

A phantom is a crystal that has had some impurity drop on it during growth, but then continues to grow right around the impurity.

Either of these types of crystal can help you heal after being hurt, or help to heal from emotional injuries. These are important crystals that will usually come into your life at a time when you are carrying a lot of pain. Just sitting with this crystal may well help you deal with pain more effectively.

TRIGGER CRYSTALS

Has a smaller crystal growing out from them. This 'trigger' can be gently squeezed to activate the power of the crystal and strengthen its attributes.

These can be used for a surge of a particular kind of energy.

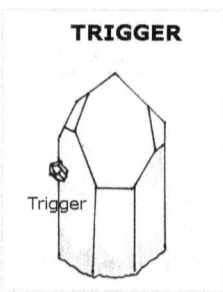

TWIN CRYSTALS II

Have two terminations (points) at the same end, which have developed from a single base. You can tell a twin crystal from two crystals that are simply attached to each other, by the fact that both parts of a twin crystal are exactly parallel to each other, and have no boundary between them in at least a small region of the crystal. These are wonderful crystals to use when dealing with 'relationship' issues. They can help you gain insight into the underlying problems in a relationship, and help work through them. They can also generate very positive energy towards improving a relationship. This works for any kind of relationship, not only man-women relationships. A twin with a rainbow can be very effectively used to project healing energy into a relationship or to keep a good relationship strong.

When you are having a problem with a relationship sit quietly with the twin and ask for help. Remember that answers come from many directions.

Twins are personal crystals as one of the twins is very closely tuned to your energy, so it is not possible to use this crystal to work for others in relationship matters.

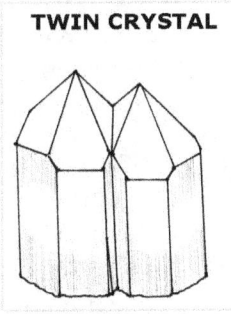
TWIN CRYSTAL

WINDOW CRYSTALS ◊

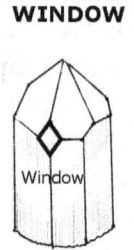

Has a small diamond shaped face which takes the place of one of the corners where two of the parallel faces usually meet the corresponding two sloping faces. Window crystals are introspective crystals in that they help you see what is inside yourself. They help bring things to the surface so you can see them and effectively deal with them. If you are having problems and aren't sure why, a window crystal can be a good help.

Window crystals are used for working within yourself to deal with problems and changes that must be made in your life. They can be used in meditation to help you solve problems that are troubling your inner being. For example, if you are very jealous of a friend, you can use a window crystal to work within yourself to find the reason and deal with it.

Think of a window crystal as a window into your soul. These are very personal crystals, and when one comes into your hands, it is intended to help you specifically.

EXERCISE: Sit with the crystal in your hand and concentrate on whatever there is within you that needs dealing with or changing. Just sit quietly and allow your mind to go where it wants to go. If you aren't sure what changes you need to make, sit with the crystal and ask it directly to help you find the areas in your life that may be causing you problems that you are not aware of.

This crystal can be used when trying to help someone else solve problems. If a friend comes to you to talk about a problem have him hold the window crystal while you talk. It can help him open up. [Take care of any energy transfer, and remember to release energetic connections at the end of the session.]

New Crystal Codes

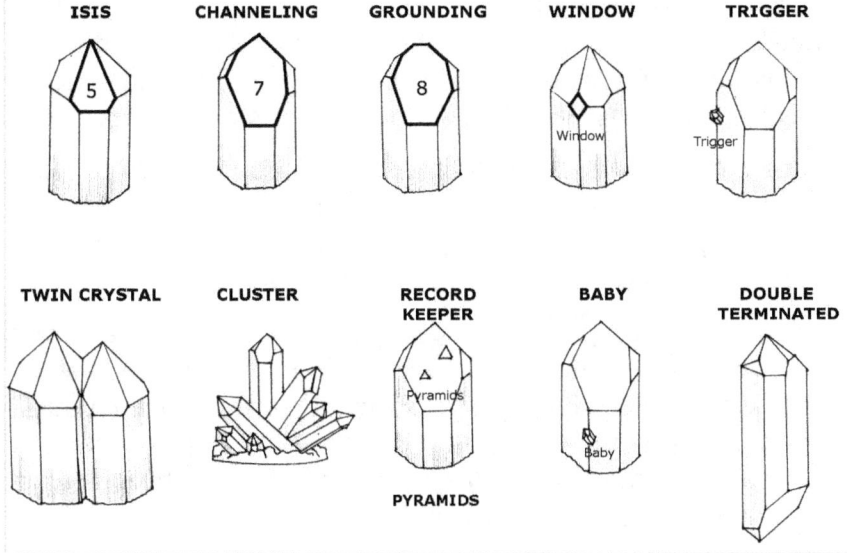

Crystal Sets

Crystals Grid Sets and Crystal Healing Sets or Crystal Focus Sets are groups of stones that can work together for a particular purpose.

Sets of stones can also be used for healing and/or manifestation purposes. You can place them as appropriate for your own healing. Intuiting or self-testing as in kinesiology will show you the best placements.

When using the crystals and stones for healing others (Crystals Grid Sets and Crystal Healing Sets), they can be placed upon the client in a grid or pattern. Or they may be placed below the client or around him or her.

Allow your intuition to inspire you and use them as your Divine Source guides you. Kinesiology or muscle testing can assist with identifying the most appropriate layouts. In my book on Energy Fields (in my Energy Secrets series) you will find an easy technique to self-test using a simple finger test – with very easy instructions.

When I use crystal grids or layouts I usually also work with the causes of the imbalances. But for those who don't know how, this is a good way to clear and alleviate difficult energies.

Remember to clear and clean before use, and to always, always clean the stones after use!!!

Following are some sets for specific uses.

Crystal Set for Love

The energies of stones have been used for ages to attract and hold love. This set is a designed to be a small, portable group for enhancing one's ability to attract and hold love.

> **Pink Manganocalcite** is a stone of universal love
>
> **Rose quartz** is the love stone
>
> **Ruby** is for romantic love (can be in rough form)
>
> **Black Onyx** is to ground love in reality
>
> **Quartz** (2 pieces) boost the energies of the other stones.

This set of stones can be carried in your pocket or kept on your desk – you can touch or run your fingers through them whilst holding thoughts of being loved or happily coupled – focusing your thoughts on a positive and happy outcome will allow these vibrations to be greatly enhanced by the quartz crystal energies, as you maintain contact with the gems at the same time.

Be aware that ruby may overstimulate sensitive types, in which case you can substitute Rhodochrocite which enhances self-identity in a loving way.

I have found in particular that the Pink Manganocalcite is a very tactile and gently powerful stone.

When using as placements or grid stone arrays, it will follow that the Black Onyx will be placed near the feet or Earth Star, or near the base chakra, whilst the pink stones will be best placed on or around the heart or shoulder areas.

The quartz crystals may be placed around the outside of the body, pointing outwards to expel unwanted old energies, or pointed inwards to support and energise the energy bodies.

Other crystals that support working with love issues are:

More Crystals For Love
      Amethyst
      Morganite (Pink Beryl)
      Rhodochrosite
      Topaz

Crystal Set for Protection

We occasionally may feel a need for some added support or energetic protection - maybe from negativity, from psychic attacks, or from general harm. With a protection set to assist with the focus one's intent about protection, we may often feel safer and somewhat relieved that our energy fields have some extra support. Here is a protection set that is a small and portable for protection of all kinds.

> **Amethyst** (2 pieces) for psychic protection
>
> **Snowflake Obsidian** (2 pieces) for protection from evil intent
>
> **Black Tourmaline** for protection from evil intent
>
> **Aventurine** (2 pieces) to clear emotional blocks and to center
>
> **Carnelian** (2 pieces) for general protection
>
> **Hematite** for staying grounded and able to receive protection
>
> **Clear Quartz** (2 pieces) to boost the energies of the other stones.

As with the previous gem stone sets, the stones can be carried in your pockets, or kept close by or on your desk so as to run your fingers through them, or in some way to come into contact with them. Wearing jewellery made out of one or more of these gems will also assist your energy fields. A friend of mine has a Hematite ring which she wears when she feels the need for extra protection and grounding, together with some Amethyst earrings - and then she carries small pebbles of the other stones in a little bag in her pocket, putting her fingers amongst the stones whenever she remembers.

Remember to clean and clear your stones regularly when using them this way.

When using these crystals in a healing grid to treat an **overwhelm of toxic energies,** I would suggest that you place the Amethyst next to the ears as close as possible, with the Snowflake Obsidian on the solar plexus, the Black Tourmaline on or close to the navel, the aventurine near the heart and/or liver, the carnelian near the solar plexus or kidneys, the Hematite near the knees or held in the hands, whilst the clear quartz is placed as described earlier.

It is always wise to work on the causes of the negative overwhelm as well as to clear the toxic energies that have been absorbed.

More Crystals for Protection

Other crystals that are appropriate for Protection include:

- Aquamarine
- Azeztulite
- Boji Stones
- Chevron Amethyst
- Fire Agate
- Labradorite
- Lapis Lazuli
- Tigers Eye
- Tourmaline
- Turquoise
- Yellow Jasper

Crystal Set for Stress Relief

We all tend to have too much stress these days, and sometimes need all the help we can get to get rid of it. This group of stones is suitable as a small portable set for stress relief.

> **Hematite** helps ground excess and chaotic energy
>
> **Lepidolite** imparts calmness - excellent for supporting the nervous system and the brain
>
> **Rubellite** (Pink Tourmaline) helps to ground, strengthen and rejuvenate

As with the previous gem stone sets, the stones can be carried in your pockets, or kept close by or on your desk so as to run your fingers through them, or in some way to come into contact with them. Wearing jewellery made out of one or more of these gems will also assist to de-stress your energy fields.

A handy and fun way of using them to relieve stress is to place them on the floor and rub your bare or stocking feet over them.

When used in a healing array, the placements can be as follows: the Hematite can be held in the hand or placed near the navel or earth star, the Lepidolite can be placed on the thymus or even the solar plexus, or held in the hand, whilst the Pink Tourmaline is good placed on the navel or heart or thymus.

Here again, Kinesiology or muscle testing can assist with identifying the most appropriate layouts.

Other crystals that can support stress and its ramifications are:

Crystals For Depression
> Botswana Agate
> Sunstone

Crystals For Nervous System
> Amazonite
> Atacamite
> Blue Lace Agate
> Cerussite
> Dendritic Agate
> Morganite

Crystals For Geopathic/EMF Smog/ Cell Phones
> Amazonite
> Aragonite
> Aventurine

Crystal Set for Success

This set of tumbled stones is metaphysically oriented to helping one gain success, particularly in one's work.

> **Citrine** is called the "success stone" because it brings success and abundance
>
> **Aventurine** is a stone that specifically brings career success
>
> **Dumortierite or Blue Quartz** enhances one's organisational abilities
>
> **Botswana agate** has the ability to assist to focus on solutions rather than problem
>
> **Clear quartz** helps pull together and magnify all these energies to create an energetic atmosphere for success.

As with the previous gem stone sets, the stones can be carried in your pockets, or kept close by or on your desk so as to run your fingers through them, or in some way to come into contact with them.

When used in a healing grid, I find Citrine is best placed near the head as it can help clear the mental body and thoughtforms that have accumulated in the etheric and near the brain and eyes (and Psychic Body), and I often use one on either side of the head. Dumortierite can be placed near the throat, neck, shoulders or even third eye, whilst the Botswana agate is good for the third eye or throat or thyroid. Again, the quartz crystal (you may choose to use two in a healing grid) may be placed around the outside of the body, pointing outwards to expel unwanted old energies, or pointed inwards to support and energise the energy bodies.

45 Crystals - Quick Reference

There are indeed thousands of different types of crystals and many, many books already written about them. Crystal information can be huge, so a useable summary can be helpful possibly narrowing down options to a manageable choice or collection.

This section is for the reader's quick and easy reference to the individual crystals quoted in the pages of this book.

Also included are crystals that I have personally found to be the most useful or that I tend to favour in my general practice.

1. Amazonite

Amazonite is a lovely creamy blue, aqua or mint green stone often streaked with white. Some varieties are pale green to dark green, aqua green or bluish green, and appear as translucent to opaque. Generally opalescent with veins, it is an extremely soothing crystal.

This gentle stone is believed to calm the brain and support the nervous system and is excellent for stress relief. Amazonite is said to soothe and dispel negative energy, aggravation and emotional trauma, and to ease irritations.

Amazonite will enhance loving communication and dispel blockages in the nervous system. It assists in communicating truth, with balance, honor and integrity. It is said to be great for non-verbal expression, and can assist the user to see different sides of the same issue or problem and so better analyse and sort the relevant information. It is also considered to be a good stone for writers and artists as it is thought to enhance one's self-expression and creativity.

It improves confidence, leadership and all aspects of communication, some recommend to wear or carry some if one has to face a challenging situation, has a difficult question to ask or is to speak in public.

Amazonite is useful if the user is caught up in one side of a disagreement, helping them to broaden their perception and to assist them in seeing different sides of the same issue. It also assists to treat feelings of social inadequacy, and soothes emotional trauma.

It is said to balance both masculine and feminine energies together more comfortably within the being. It is also able to better enhance one's masculine qualities toward a better expression. Amazonite will also balance differing personality traits and help to reduce self-damaging behavior.

Amazonite assists with self-expression, artistic creativity and is good for anyone involved in the arts for besides its gifts in communication of ideas and concepts, it increases self-respect, grace, confidence and, self-assuredness. The pale green variety is said to be instrumental in distilling the raw information used for personal expression.

It is said to enhance intuition, integrity, honor, creativity, intellect, psychic powers and ability and it brings psychic blessings.

Amazonite is said to align the physical and astral bodies. It aids in the alignment of the mental and etheric bodies and brings joy and upliftment.

It also facilitates a clearer vision of one's own harmful tendencies and thus makes these easier to acknowledge and release. It is known for its abilities to balance energy, engender harmony and to align one with universal love.

Amazonite is recognised as a "Stone of Abundance and success" and is said to attract good luck and prosperity. It has been used to bring in new business by placing some over a door.

Physically, it can help with issues associated with the throat, sinus, chest and lungs. It is believed that when used in crystal or energy healing Amazonite is able to heal emotional disturbances and the after effects of emotional trauma.

It is also reputed to have spiritual energy healing powers of preventative energy that will enhance one's health in general, and that its energies can benefit and aid with colic, as well as decreasing heart problems, benefitting the muscles, calcium deficiency, pregnancy, eczema, muscle cramps, the nervous system, lessen tooth decay and osteoporosis.

It is a good energy filter and is said to block geopathic stress from computers and microwaves, cell phone emanations and alleviate electromagnetic smog and pollution. It also brings soothing energies to these emanations and aggravations.

The Chakras it is associated with most are the Heart and Throat, Third Eye, Thymus and Solar Plexus Chakras, though it also soothes and calms all of the Chakras.

It is said to be a wonderful assistance for a peaceful transition of the dying out of this life and bringing them closer to the Divine.

Amazonite keywords include: Life Force, Creative Expression, "Stone of Abundance and Success".

2. Amethyst

Amethyst is a beautifully coloured quartz crystal and ranges from violet to dark purples, with some rarer varieties of lavender amethyst as well as rare green amethyst. It has been connected with balance and psychic abilities, and also balance of psychic abilities. Related to all things spiritual, it assists in healing body, mind and soul in a holistic way.

Amethyst has long been called the "sobriety stone." Amethyst is very well known since the ancients to prevent drunkenness. In ancient Rome, crushed amethyst was added to wine cups to prevent drunkenness. Others fashioned Amethyst into a drinking vessel, because of this belief. It has been used for millennia to assist with healing alcoholism, drugs, smoking, destructive compulsive behaviours, and addictions of all kinds. It is and was used to recover from both physical addictions as well as addictive relationships. As the ancient detoxifier, it is also claimed to assist with clearing poisons.

Amethyst is a calming stone which works on the emotional, spiritual, and physical planes to bring energies in mystical realms to the physical of stability, peace, calm, balance, courage and inner strength.

Amethyst raises one's vibrations to a more spiritual level or frequency. It is good for those who strongly resist any interference with their personal freedom to make their own decisions and plans. This crystal is also good for individuals experiencing low self-esteem, and helps one to feel more integrated within society. Amethyst also assists in bringing peace into love relationships.

It has also been used to help ease the pain of grief, and promote happiness.

Amethyst is beneficial when dealing with legal problems, and money issues. This can lead to prosperity and abundance. Amethyst is also protection for travelers.

Amethyst aids to heal personal losses and grief, bringing one gently back from the past and into the present. It has a gently sedative energy that can promote peacefulness, happiness, and contentment. It is also said to bring emotional stability and inner strength. This stability and strength not only helps one hold firm in one's life, but it can enhance flexibility and cooperation as to be flexible when required is a sure sign of strength.

Spiritually, it enhances meditation and an awareness of God. Amethyst can increase intuition, and integrate the emotional, mental, and integrated spiritual bodies especially when there is a sense of un-centeredness, or hyper-kinetic activity. Amethyst is said to help one open to communication with angels, or increase telepathy and other psychic abilities. It is thus an excellent stone for dream work and dream recall, past life work, and to help one see one's path.

It is good to use for clearing the energy fields when held in the hand at night as part of an energy clearing process. Soothing to the nervous system, it can aid in smoothing transmissions of neural signals and ease the nervous system. This also can aid in dispelling rage, anger, fear and anxiety.

Amethyst is a very powerful and protective crystal, and is a first choice of many metaphysicians. It is a natural stress reliever. It assists with psychic and spiritual protection and excels at the purification and transformation of Negative Energies. It has also been used in metaphysical work as well as in crystal healing to clear psychic attacks.

In the psychic and spiritual realms, amethyst is an excellent all-purpose stone that can increase spirituality and enhance intuition and psychic powers of all kinds. It does this by making a clear connection between the earth plane and other planes and worlds. Amethyst is not only a psychic protection stone, but is also used to protect one from thieves, and to protect travelers.

Amethyst brings stability, peace, calm, and balance. It engenders courage and inner strength and supports self esteem.

Physically Amethyst is used to heal the withdrawal symptoms of any sort of addiction, and helps with headaches, insomnia, arthritis, pain relief, circulatory system issues, endocrine system problems, chronic fatigue, fibro-myalgia, immune system deficiencies, and general healing.

Amethyst geodes are wonderful for collecting energy and focusing it. Also for clearing other crystals as well as for space clearing.

Good Keywords for Amethyst are: Psychic Protection, Purification, Well-Being and Peace, "Stone of Sobriety", Spirituality.

3. Apophyllite Pyramids

Apophyllite crystals grow in pyramid shapes naturally. These pyramidal forms can be transparent, cloudy white, green, yellowish or pale peach coloured. The pyramids can often be striated. Green is said by some to be the most powerful, but they are an adjunct to work with any other crystal, amplifying their energies similarly to quartz. However, they are very powerful in their own right. Some pyramids or crystal formations appear to have mirrors within, and these reflective qualities enhance the energetic actions of this stone.

It has been used for centuries in India in the "art of gazing". It is understood that in most families one Mirror Apophyllite is usually passed down from generation to generation. It is often called upon to reflect the doings from the past to its user, in order to see both the good and the bad aspects of a families' past. This is to allow the gazer to be aware of and work on improving the deficiencies from within. It provides a clear and absolute connection between the physical bodies and the astral bodies of its user. Mirror Apophyllite is an extremely powerful crystal and will also enrich the users' intuitive capacities by stimulating the Third Eye Chakra.

Apophyllite is also associated with the crown Chakra. It is an aid to meditation and can help make a conscious connection with the spiritual world. It has reportedly been used to help in fire-walking and astral travel. It helps one see the truth and then act on it, and is an energy stimulator. This stone can assist one in tapping into the creative forces and bringing them into manifestation form with great joy. The energy of this crystal can connect people with nature and the nature spirits. Personal transformation also becomes more playful.

Apophyllite can also benefit the physical eyes for it can relieve tired eyes when placed on the eyelids. When placed on the third eye Chakra, it is said to enhance clairvoyance and mystical vision. Used as a 'gazing' tool such as a crystal globe, it can assist the sensitive or psychic to look into the future. It can also stimulate intuitive vision when placed on third eye.

Emotionally, Apophyllite can aid to release suppressed emotions. It can calm apprehension, overcome anxiety, worries and fears and can help one to tolerate uncertainty. It calms and grounds the spirit and helps the body to feel more comfortable with one's spiritual connections. It creates a conscious connection between the physical and the spiritual realms.

This is a stone of truth and promotes introspection into one's own behavior and past, helping to cut through and abandon pretence and reserve. It brings recognition of one's true self and feels more comfortable in the revealing of this to the world.

It is an effective stress reducer, helping to release negative thought patterns and to deal with and release mental blockages. This can result in lessening attachment, and because it also imbues the thought processes with universal love, it makes decision making more congruent with one's spirit and therefore easier.

It has a connection with the Akashic Record, enabling past life issues to be accessed and dealt with more easily.

Keywords for Apophyllite Pyramids are: Joy, "Stone of Truth", Past Records.

4. Aquamarine

Aquamarine is a beautiful transparent form of Beryl and it can range in colour through palest blues and blue-greens to turquoise. Legend has it that it is the treasure of mermaids and that in ancient times sailors would carry Aquamarine to protect them from drowning and to promote safe sea travel. Aquamarine resonates to the energy of the ocean, helping the holder to connect with the nature spirits of the sea.

Aquamarine is often known as a "Stone of Courage and Protection" and gives a fortitude that can bring great power. It is said to assist with quick intellectual response. Because of its soothing energy Aquamarine makes it a perfect companion to calm fears and phobias.

Aquamarine is used to help with reasoning and promote logic, effectively encouraging the thinking process and better clarity of thought. Aquamarine can also aid in the assimilation of new knowledge, making it a great crystal for students of all kinds. It also encourages intellectual growth and the desire and accumulation of inner knowledge. This can assist to bring an opening up for connection to one's intuition and the super-conscious mind.

Aquamarine is also used to align all of the Chakras and enhance the aura. Used often with the Throat Chakra, Aquamarine can be used to promote verbal self-expression. It can also work with the Heart Chakra by helping one to realize their innermost truth.

The metaphysical properties of Aquamarine make it an excellent stone for the spiritual initiate. It is used to enhance and further spiritual communication and clear any communication blocks. Aquamarine can calm and reduce fear and worry by opening the mind up to understanding the nature of Divine Perfection in the Universe.

Aquamarine helps to facilitate the releasing of old patterns of behaviour that no longer serve, and that can actually inhibit one's growth. Aquamarine brings peace and calm to the overactive mind, making it a great aid for deepening meditation and is said to reveal new insights from one's higher self that can be applied in daily life. Aquamarine is believed to give strength to deal with difficult situations and to allow you to stay focused under pressure.

Aquamarine is often used to enhance one's intellectual prowess, helping one to think quickly to come up with solutions with little warning. Carrying Aquamarine on one's person can help to remind the individual to be prepared for most any scenario that could be encountered, given the current set of circumstances.

Aquamarine allows one to look at emotional situations from other viewpoints and perspectives. Because it can help overcome judgment of others, it helps to encourage tolerance.

This stone can enhance and develop a greater sensitivity and in this way it can initiate a greater connection with the experience of a mass or global consciousness. It is also said to aid in bringing one into a real flow in life, enhancing the experience of continuity during one's existence.

Metaphysically it brings inner peace and self-love, gives shielding for the aura, and is said to bring angels for their guidance and protection. As mentioned, it is therefore an excellent crystal for meditation. Aquamarine is used metaphysically to dispel anger and fear. It can also be used psychically to do past life recall and work.

Aquamarine is also said to be a wonderful good luck stone.

In crystal energy healing Aquamarine has been used for healing GERD*, intestinal disorders, chronic fatigue, the endocrine system, eyes and eyesight, fluid retention, headaches, the nervous system, phobias, and teeth and gums.

Physically it is said that placing Aquamarine on the throat Chakra or area is believed to help alleviate problems of the throat, swollen glands and the thyroid.

Keywords: "Stone of Courage and Protection", Communication, Calmness, Luck.

*GERD: Gastroesophageal reflux disease is a chronic digestive disease.

5. Aragonite

Aragonite can come in clumps of sputnik-like formations connected together, or like a Star cluster of crystals radiating out from a central core, though the columnar shapes all end with flattened tops instead of sharp points like quartz crystal points. Aragonite can also appear in caves in the form of stalactites and "cave flowers" as well as in deposits on the seabed in various locations.

Their unique structure, with many outward pointing crystals distribute energy and light outwards, this can create an amazing energetic charge.

Aragonite occurs in various colours that include white, gray, reddish, yellow-green and blue, though the most commonly recognized is the reddish star clusters from Morocco and the larger and more purplish orthorhombic crystals found in Molina de Aragon in Spain. Which is from where it derives its name. The more recent blue specimens are from China.

In crystal and energy healing Aragonite is thought to encourage feelings of self-worth and confidence.

Aragonite increases energy, in particular the energy of prayers and positive intent. Though it is also helpful for people who are considered airy-fairy or "off with the fairies" to knuckle down and to stay focused. It encourages tolerance and flexibility to a tired mind. Aragonite supports those who feel they have too much responsibility, providing them with the necessary strength and support. This aids one to combat anger and frustration.

It aids to assist with an increase in energy to overcome stress, stabilising energy and enabling one to ground during stressful times.

Aragonite is an excellent earth healer and a spiritually grounding stone attuned to Gaia. It can assist to transform geopathic stress and clear blockages, deepening one's connection with the earth. It is also a useful stone for EMF smog and electronic interferences such as cell phones etc.

Aragonite teaches and enhances patience, acceptance and the ability to take on more responsibility, and it strengthens reliability and practicality. It is said to reduce anger and also to raise one's energy levels in order to help clear and focus the mind so that one can concentrate on whatever task is at hand.

These are strong healing stones to help with emotional problems, such as anxiety caused through stress. They are also considered a good crystal to work with to clear energy blockages that originate in past lives. It is able to stabilise spiritual development, helping one to gain insights to the causes of problems and situations.

It is also thought to be symbolic of the importance of symmetry in nature, and suggests progressions from the singular to the universal. Aragonite can help provide one with insight when confronting problems on several simultaneous levels.

Metaphysically is it said to boost self-confidence and feelings of self-worth. It can assist to diminish anger and relieve stress, and it enhances the functions of the Base Chakra, Sacral Chakra and the Earth Star and Earthing Chakras.

Physically, it is professed by some to be beneficial for not only chronic fatigue, as they assist one to feel more physically energized, but also for hair loss.

It is also called "The Conservationist's Stone". It is known to be used as aquarium sand due to its abilities when used from the aragonite that forms in the ocean and in caves as inorganic precipitates called marine cements. Large deposits of this calcium carbonate oolitic aragonite sand are found on the seabed in the Bahamas and are perfect for filtering and supporting aquatic life.

Good keywords for Aragonite include: Increase Energy, "The Conservationist's Stone", Patience and Reliability.

6. Atacamite

Atacamite is a relatively new discovery crystal and its properties are still being explored. It comes as a brilliant green to deep turquoise color and has been mistaken for a version of Chrysocolla though it may well share some of the properties of that crystal. Atacamite is made up of tiny crystal structures on a binding matrix and contains copper, which even though it a necessarily micronutrient can cause copper toxicity in large amounts. Therefore great care and knowledge should be used when attempting to make gem elixirs.

This crystal formation and its minerals have a powerful Lemurian vibration and may have revealed itself to assist the planet and humanity in getting through these unsettling times. Atacamite is certainly becoming known as a crystal with powerful energy and relevant to these current times.

Atacamite seems to more and more popular for use as a stone for spiritual connection and for associated various psychic and mystical practices such as meditation and higher spiritual guidance. Thus it is considered a stone of visualization. It has also been used for astral travel, but in these times of melting of inter-dimensional barriers one needs to take great care and be aware of the pitfalls of this practice until the energy shifts have settled again. Not everyone is equipped to navigate back safely from astral levels which occupy different vibrations, levels and energies   Nor know how to contain the various dimensional accesses afterwards.

At a broader level, it can be used for emotional healing, and to expand one's ability to show one's love. It can also be used as a protection stone and help keep harm away. It has an impressive nature and can be used to enhance motivation and optimism during trying times.

Atacamite is a powerful third eye Chakra stone, and also works on the Crown, heart and lower Chakras.

Meditation with this stone can bring powerful visual images and it may forcefully open the third eye, so care should be used not to push too quickly and to maintain balance. Yet even though it is forceful in this regard it can also intensify one's ability to make a connection to one's guides and higher self.

It is said to heal the spirit, while providing a soothing energy and bringing a peaceful state of mind.

Atacamite is excellent when used for removing energy blockages. Besides which it can be used to enhance motivation and optimism during trying times., so is well equipped for those on a spiritual journey.

Physically, Atacamite is used in crystal healing and energy work for thyroid, fertility, nervous system, gonads and the heart.

The nervous system is particularly benefited by the clarity of this stone's vibrations, and old stresses are relieved and soothed.

Some say that this crystal has a primary use for the tubercular and gonorrhea miasms and may alleviate a whole range of physical difficulties within the lower Chakras.

Atacamite is associated primarily with the heart Chakra due to its higher vibration of turquoise, which is a color of the new Era, promoting global understandings and advancements in consciousness.

It also aids in restoring lost spiritual trust.

Keywords for Atacamite are: Visualisation, Spirituality, Consciousness.

7. Aventurine

Aventurine is a variety of quartz and tends to opaqueness. Green is the most common colour in this crystal, but it also comes in blue, red, yellow, brown or peach. It can also appear to have tiny speckles. It is a favourite for use in energy healing and these are heart Chakra stones that will release anxiety, and create optimism and love of life, the green in particular. The Aventurines also work well with other related Chakra depending on their associated colours.

It supports the Heart Chakra and aligns to Universal Love. It works to clear emotional blocks and to help center oneself. Emotional Tranquility is a key action and this helps relieve anxiety.

Aventurine stimulates the mind and motivation. It assists to foster a sense of independence and also helps to activate and expand one's creativity. It is a stone of prosperity, assisting issues around mental rigidity, high mindedness, pride and aloofness.

Aventurine brings career success and aids one to manifest prosperity and good luck. It will help in dealing with inner child anxiety and issues related to childhood and caused by poor parenting or associated problems. It particularly assists in alleviating anxiety and buried fears originating during the first seven years of childhood.

When used in psychotherapy, Aventurine assists in the development of emotional tranquility and a more positive attitude toward life. This increases the frequency required for advancing and fostering friendships and success.

Aventurine promotes a positive, easy going attitude towards life, and balances the male and female energies. It also purifies the physical, mental and emotional bodies, this helps to align one's centers and effectively promoting health and well being. It aids in releasing fear, anxiety and stress, and is an aid regarding sleep disorders.

Aventurine benefits one in all areas of creativity, and imagination, as well as intellect and mental clarity. It enhances prosperity and brings career success. It is a gentle stone that gives a sense of calm and balance and enhances happiness.

It helps one to see alternatives and potentials in all situations, giving a positive outlook, courage and inner strength. It also brings luck, especially in games of chance. Aventurine promotes compassion and empathy, calming one's anger, and it also brings joy, happiness and emotional tranquility.

It is a stone of Protection and Aventurine serves to protect us against electromagnetic energy and environmental pollution.

Physically it is beneficial for blood, circulatory system and general health. Aventurine stimulates healing of the muscles and bones, assists in relieving headaches and migraines and helps blood pressure and cholesterol. It is also said to help protect against heart conditions and inflammation.

It is also recommended for stress and environmental relief such as Geopathic toxicities, EMF Smog and Cell Phones.

Keywords for Aventurine are Prosperity, Career Success, Heart Flow, Emotional Tranquility.

8. Azeztulite

This variety of quartz crystal is colourless or white and tends toward being opaque. Azeztulite is a particularly high vibrational type of quartz. It is also the name given to a cloudy quartz found on a remote mountain in North Carolina. Unlike regular prismatic Quartz crystals, it is cloudy in appearance and is said to form in small irregular shapes and clusters.

I have also heard that the name Azeztulite is claimed to have been channeled by a writer of crystal books but at this time I do not yet know this for fact.

There is also a crystal called Satyaloka that is said to be a variety of this same Quartz which is gathered in ritual by the monks around the Satyaloka monastery in Southern India. This particular type of Quartz is also said to carry a very high vibration of spiritual enlightenment and it is referred to as Satyaloka Azeztulite. The monks of the Satyaloka monastery say that the pure spiritual energies which permeate the area of their monastery are also carried by these crystals. They also believe that spiritual beings from higher dimensions are assisting humanity through the energy of these stones.

In all cases this crystal is said to be a tool for spreading enlightenment throughout the world. I cannot confirm that this is true, but I am very aware that this is an extremely powerful and spiritual crystal that can help to open dimensional doorways, even access to a time-space tunnel – so it should be used with great care for this purpose as not many know how to manage these accesses safely.

Care should be taken when working in interdimensional realms and with higher spiritual spheres if one is not used to these very high vibrations.

I know from experience how important it is to allow the time and dedication required when faced with the challenges one meets on such a spiritual journey. It can task one's physical energies or create toxic releases or cause even more disorienting issues, so initial use and approaches should be taken in small steps, whilst also learning about how to manage the associated energies and vibrational shifts safely and with great respect. This crystal requires respect and esteem.

However, as one works with it, one's vibration can also lift, bringing a positive and transforming vibration.

The energy and vibrational shifts can be extremely powerful and may well have unpleasant side effects, so use in small segments or doses and always use a supporting crystal such as Aquamarine and Ametrine (a combination of Amethyst and Citrine crystal) to assist with assimilation and integration.

Its vibration is believed to be of extra-terrestrial origin, and like most quartz, has the ability to enhance one's spiritual growth quickly once one has committed to working with it.

Some crystals take some time to adapt to, especially very high vibration varieties of quartz. It is certainly an aid to boosting humanity to the next level of consciousness and evolution.

On a more mundane level, and almost needless to say after what has just been stated, is that it is excellent for centering the self and to clear emotional blocks.

It is said that Azeztulite doesn't need cleansing like normal quartz normally does because it does not absorb negativity. However I am a firm believer in not overtasking any stone and in ensuring that all crystals receive and probably benefit from regular cleansings.

Keywords for Azeztulite are: Interdimensional, Consciousness Shift.

9. Black Onyx

Onyx is generally, though not always, a shiny stone and its mostly found as black pebbles or carved into shapes, points or jewelry. In its raw form it comes in rough dull chunks. There are often flecks, bands or streaks in the stone that can create a marble effect, usually gray or white, but there may also be other colours. It has a smooth beauty when polished and smoothed.

Black Onyx is powerful protection stone, and is able to absorb and transform negative energy, helping to prevent the draining away of personal energy. It is the stone to use when dealing with tragedy.

Black Onyx aids the development of emotional and physical strength and stamina, especially when support is needed during times of stress, confusion or grief.

It assists with the challenges of life, especially those caused by a drain of energy. can be used for protection from such. It also helps with grounding and controlling or eliminating excess or unwanted energies.

Black Onyx fosters wise decision-making and is a good stone to have around during times of mental or physical stress or bereavement, as it provides strength and support during difficult circumstances.

Black Onyx is believed to promote stamina and vigour and can be used to encourage happiness and good fortune. It is also said to promote self-control by helping the wearer to better handle excessive emotions and passions.

Black Onyx is a strength-giving stone and can provide support for self-discipline issues. Because it helps to hold physical memories, Black Onyx can be useful in healing old wounds or past life issues.

This Onyx is a soothing stone that is said to help alleviate fears and worries and to help one to feel comfortable within the self and in one's surroundings. It is also believed to promote stamina and vigour and to encourage the making of wise decisions. It also helps to balance an overactive sex drive as it can absorb and flatten emotional intensity, and provide the strength required to maintain self control.

Black Onyx is a strength-giving stone and besides providing support for self-discipline issues, it can also be useful in healing old wounds or past life issues. Black Onyx absorbs negativity, protects from harm, and encourages self control when seeking some form of abstention.

The shapes or patterns that Onyx holds inside it have led some to believe that Onyx has a picture in it that tells a story or carries a lesson. Interestingly, Onyx can retain the memory of physical occurrences surrounding a person. Consequently it is a strong stone to use in psychometry because it can tell the story of the wearer.

Spiritually this is a great stone for past life work as it can heal old injuries that have their roots in past life trauma. The crystal properties can also aid in the healing of old grief or sorrow from other lives or this one. Black Onyx provides a feeling of strength and can assist when going through stressful circumstances, encouraging calmness when feeling stressed or anxious.

Onyx is associated primarily with the root Chakra and assists with grounding love into reality. Black Onyx is also able to promote fidelity.

Black Onyx and Red Onyx are associated with the Base Chakra. White Onyx is associated with linking the Base and Crown Chakras to have balanced energy throughout the Chakra system. Other colors are associated with the relevant Chakra color.

Keywords for Black Onyx are: Strength-Giver, Emotional Grounder, Psychometry.

10. Black Tourmaline

Black Tourmaline conveys all of the properties listed in the Tourmaline section and is particularly valued for its abilities with protection from evil intent.

It is a solid feeling striated crystal, and is an extremely dense and usually shiny black. It is found in shards or wands and polished pebbles as well as lending itself to jewelry.

It assists restlessness and is a valuable stone for crises and for periods of extreme stress, bringing good grounding abilities whilst helping to repel negative energies.

It is suggested to carry this stone when you feel surrounded by negativity or are dealing with extreme stress. It supports the body's electromagnetic field, allowing for better function when facing challenge.

One of Black Tourmaline's better known qualities is its capacity regarding Protection (especially from Evil Intent).

Black Tourmaline does not absorb negative energy but repels it and further transmutes lower frequency thoughts or energy to a higher frequency of light. It aids in bringing in more light and spiritual energy into the physical realms. It radiates light and protection for the wearer, providing psychic protection as well as good grounding for the spiritually aware.

This stone is very helpful for the release of painful emotions, as it promotes strength and courage, and it supports the nervous system and circulation.

It is good for supporting detoxification processes too as it helps clear the etheric bodies in tandem with the clearing on the physical and cellular levels.

Keywords for Black Tourmaline include: Protection (especially from Evil Intent), Transformation, Grounding, Clearing, Balancing.

11. Blue Lace Agate

Blue Lace Agate is a beautifully banded stone, often appearing similar to lace in its intricate speckling and rows of quartz. It is always a pale blue and has white or darker blues and even apparently transparent layers in banding formations. It is often seen in tumbled stones and has a very calming and soothing quality.

Agates foster love, abundance, wealth, good luck, longevity, acceptance, courage, protection, balance, harmony, generosity, strength, security and appreciation of nature. That is a lot to say about any stone and this is why the banded Agates are considered very powerful stones. But they are also very calming and soothing to the emotions.

Blue Lace Agate is a very cooling and soothing crystal, bringing calmness that endows one with a gentle sense of peace and tranquility.

Considered to be a major emotional soother and healer, it also works on self expression particularly assisting one to contact and experience the verbal expression of their thoughts and feelings. The Throat Chakra is nurtured and supported and anger and anxieties are neutralized. It assists one to see all the beauty one's eyes touch.

Blue Lace Agate also can assist with the expression of thoughts and feelings and in the process of breaking down negative or harsh pictures or images of oneself, without further judgment. It is excellent in supporting the nervous system and in stress relief.

This gentle crystal can bring about a deeper spiritual connection, enhancing one's modes of expression and assisting with making quicker decisions. The addiction or tendency to over-think can be neutralized and eased. It is also beneficial for couples, assisting them in communication issues.

The energy of Blue Lace Agate contains the qualities of grace and movement. This can support performers or speaker, and can help one with being at one with their audience.

Spiritually this crystal is highly inspirational when working with the inner self and also works well with the Heart, Third Eye and Crown Chakra, besides the Throat Chakra.

This crystal also helps one to focus on the inner source of love within one that can transform and heal those inner wounds. Blue Lace Agate improves one's ego and self-esteem, assisting emotional balance and strengthening one's positive personality traits.

Physically Blue Lace Agate is claimed to strengthen and accelerate the repair of bones, thyroid deficiencies and lymph infections. It can also soothe sore eyes and any skin issues associated with redness or irritation. It is also thought to aid improved or more peaceful sleep, assisting in the release of insomnia caused frustration.

Keywords for Blue Lace Agate include: Peace of Mind, Stress relief, Self Expression.

12. Boji Stones

These solid and round, grey-brown discs have a high iron component and are an ancient coalescence of separate particles of matter into one solid form. Many of the stones may contain traces of fossiliferous matter and these stones are called Concretions.

Boji Stones are said to be a container for balanced energy, and are claimed to be as old as the earth's creation itself.

It is claimed that the balanced energy joins with the elements, and the powers that formed the earth also formed the Boji. They are an Iron-magnetite concretion blend of fossil and are apparently held together by the energy within. If the energy in a stone is depleted or destroyed, the stone changes molecular structure and can become dust according to geologists.

When rubbing two Bojis together in the dark one can see sparks fly. Placed in fire they tend to explode.

If they are left on the ground the energy leaves and the stones rot away. It is said that these formations like to be held, and can die or waste away if they are not held regularly.

They are said to come in pairs of one male Boji Stone and one female Boji stone, which need to be stored apart because their magnetic-ness neutralizes each other. The "male stone is the rougher one and the "female" stone is the smooth one.

They both carry a positive and a negative charge. And are considered excellent for healing emotional problems. They carry a high level of healing and powerful grounding energy. Used in body layouts they are effective in clearing the Chakras and to bring balance to both the male and female energies within the body.

In energy work they are also said to be powerful enough to clear hypnotic commands that may have been implanted in a previous time. Because they embody spiritual grounding energy they can be helpful for spiritual development.

They are also thought to be good for clearing away outmoded, outworn and unsupportive thought patterns and learned behaviours.

Boji Stones are extremely helpful if you have been doing spiritual development work and have remained ungrounded afterwards. By holding one in each hand and feeling the weight of them pulling one's energy down again and back into the body will release all symptoms of dizziness, clumsiness, flitting thoughts, feeling like you are not in your body, light-headedness, or of not being able to hold a thought.

They are also said to be able to both take one back through the many lives of existence and progress ones thought processes forward to eternity, whilst providing both grounding and shielding of the physical, mental, and emotional bodies.

Bojis are protective stones, and they can enhance ones sense of well-being. They emanate a loving, kind, and sincere energy when held.

They are said to both balance and align the Chakras and to be helpful in the removal of energy blockages.

Their electromagnetic abilities also assist to provide for the transfer of energy from the etheric body to the physical body as well as to clean, charge, and fill the voids or holes in one's aura.

Boji Stone increases channeling abilities. All Chakras, meridians and nadis are strengthened

This stone is also considered useful with agriculture and horticulture and it helps one to attune with nature.

Better communication with plants and animals are engendered.

It is suggested that they are not used in combination with Tigers Eye or any stone containing asbestos as this can bring on a sense of ill-will.

Keywords for the Boji Stones are: "Unblocker", Attunement to Nature, Protection.

13. Botswana Agate

Botswana Agate is generally waxy in appearance, and it is predominantly banded in shades of pink and gray, though some layers can contain muted brown or apricot. Botswana Agate is a variety of banded Chalcedony, a mineral of the Quartz family.

The volcanic activity that produced these lovely stones dates back nearly 187 million years ago, and though the igneous stones of Botswana began as volcanic flow, they did not originate from the usual mountainous volcanoes. Rather the lava flowed in waves from long faults along the lower rock layers which rolled across the landscape, effectively depositing layer upon layer of Silica and Quartz. This action created the slender bandings and the subsequent patterns which make these Agates highly unique and desirable. Indeed, some collectors consider them to be the royalty of Agates.

This crystal is soo comforting and protective and is very soothing to those who are lonely, easily hurt or who are grieving a loss. It wraps its layers of gentle pinks, browns and grays around the soul like soft, warm flannel. Agate has a lesser intensity than straight out quartz and so it vibrates to a slower frequency than other stones, but is highly regarded and extremely effective as a stabilizing and strengthening influence. Agates work very gently and slowly, however they have a lasting impact. Agate tends to go to work straight on the cause, instead of the symptom of an issue.

Botswana Agate is sometimes called the "change stone" because of its property of helping one handle change in a positive way. It gently helps one make transitions of any kind in a way that change is not as difficult or painful as it could be without it. It is a comforting stone. Carrying a bit of Botswana Agate in the pocket can help one cope easily with the minor changes that life throws at us daily.

Relief from depression and/or grief is another property of Botswana agate. Botswana Agate strengthens the mind so that it has the ability to focus on solutions rather than the problem and is perfect for stress relief and depression. It also helps one to be clear about what action is required when the problem and solution has been recognised. It is excellent for balancing emotional, physical and intellectual energy, and in harmonizing the experience of the positive and negative forces of the universe. It increases creativity and productivity

Botswana Agate is helpful in overcoming addictions and other self-destructive compulsive behaviour patterns, as well as dealing with repressed emotional issues.

Botswana Agate is known as a stone of good luck and wealth. As a success stone, it helps one achieve and cope with success. It is also helpful in overcoming negative emotions by bringing love into the Chakras and is great for achieving stability and balance in many areas of one's life.

Physically, Botswana Agate is strongly recommended for fire-fighters, people who smoke, and for anyone who comes in regular contact with excessive amounts of heat or smoke. It is also helpful for anyone who wants to quit smoking.

Spiritually, it can be helpful for those who are struggling with congruency or sincerity in their lifestyle, as it promotes an understanding of the need for deeper meaning and coherence. Botswana Agate can also stimulate the exploration of the unknown and further one's quest toward a more enlightened state. Botswana Agate increases the power of one's intuition and energizes the auric body.

Many feel that Botswana Agate has an anti-depressant quality. It is beneficial to the nervous system and can help rid the body of toxins, as well as help in the healing of broken bones.

It is also a stone of sensuality. Botswana Agate can help those who have repressed emotional issues that need to be addressed so that they can release and heal. Constant love is encouraged as this stone assists to initiate and establish Universal Love.

Keywords for Botswana Agate are: Joy, Luck, Change.

14. Calcite

The word Calcite comes from the Latin word *calx*, and the Greek word *chalix*, meaning "lime". Calcite is common in limestone and marble. An alternate name is Calcspar. Generally Calcite tends to a milky translucence. Calcite can come in the clear Calcite or in milky colours of yellow, peach-orange, green, white, blue and lime green.

Clear Calcite is sometimes called Optical Calcite or Iceland Spar. Optical Calcite has a double refraction. If you lay it over a line of writing, you will see the writing show up in two lines through the Calcite.

Calcite is known for its ability to soothe and bring tranquility, especially to the spiritual heart. It can aid us in learning the hidden lessons in each situation and encounter that we come across and help to urge us to new options.

Calcites are emotionally balancing. They bring in more joy and lightness, and alleviate fear as well as reducing stress. They bring balance and amplify truth.

Calcite increases and amplifies energy. This makes it an excellent stone for distance healing, as well as other types of healing. One of the energies it amplifies is learning abilities, and thus is a great stone for students.

Calcite is a protecting, grounding and centering stone, and can help bring inner peace. Since Calcite also promotes creativity and imagination, the inner peace it can bring is a vibrant one.

Calcite has been said to increase prosperity. It can also be helpful in astral travel and in channeling, as well as increasing intuition. Calcite is also a stone of spirituality and wisdom. It can assist us to recognise duality and give clearer vision.

All Calcites are helpful in lessening of fear and reducing stress. Calcite is probably the premier cleanser of stored negative energies in the human system, and works on all levels from the physical to the etheric. This makes it a very purifying stone. It can also be used to clear negativity in the environment, such as a room that it's in.

In the realm of relationships, Calcite brings its properties of grounding and centering, to make it a stone of reconciliation. Calcite can ameliorate arguments in a relationship, and help maintain a practical balance between the people in the relationship.

Physically, Calcites are good for back pain, increasing physical strength, teeth, eyes, and are generally good for healing. Clear Calcite can be used for treating all conditions. It can also be used for detoxifying and as an antiseptic agent. Calcite is especially helpful with emotional and mental conditions.

All Calcites have the basic properties noted. For properties associated with different coloured Calcites, see the page for that particular type of Calcite.

Calcite increases and amplifies energy. It can also be helpful in astral travel and in channeling, as well as with increasing intuition. All Calcites are helpful in lessening of fear and reducing stress. Calcite is a protecting, purifying, grounding and centering stone, and can help bring inner peace. It also increases creativity, imagination, and prosperity.

Calcite is also a stone of spirituality, wisdom and reconciliation. Calcites of different colours are great for using to open and balance the various chakras. Physically, Calcites can heal back pain, increase physical strength, help to heal teeth issues, and are generally good for healing. It is strongly recommended for those involved in the healing professions. It is also able to grounds excess energy, soothing the nerves and nervous system.

<u>Clear</u> Calcite can be used to open and balance all the chakras. All Chakras, especially Crown.

<u>Green</u> Calcites help overcome addictions, heal joints, bones, kidney, bladder, and the endocrine system, relieve pain. Also helps with manifestation, abundance, and intuition. Heart Chakra.

<u>Blue</u> is particularly good for channeling and increasing energy. Third Eye, Throat and Thymus Chakras.

<u>Yellow</u> Calcite is also particularly good for Shamanic work, meditation, channeling, intuition, and amplifying energy. Solar Plexus Chakra.

<u>Pink</u> Calcite (ManganoCalcite) is a stone of love and amplifies Reiki and other universal life force energies. Heart Chakra.

<u>Orange</u> reduces chronic fatigue, and increases psychic abilities. Sacral Chakra.

<u>Red</u> brings courage and inner strength and energy to handle survival situations, and benefits sensuality/sexuality. Base Chakra.

<u>Honey</u> Calcite is also very good for increasing energy. Navel and Thymus Chakras.

<u>Optical</u> Calcite is beneficial for headaches. Crown Chakra.

Keywords: Cleansing, Reconciliation, Energy Healing, Tranquility, Joy.

15. Carnelian

Carnelian crystal is usually smoothly pebble shaped, or in smoothish chunks, and ranges from warm reds through oranges and pinky-orange to brown.

Carnelian is an agate class of chalcedony and is a stone of creativity, individuality and courage.

Carnelian is a stone of abundance, bringing a warmth and stability that helps to restore vitality and motivation again. In addition it aids in the manifestation of one's desires, and is considered to bring good luck. It aids one to achieve greater success in personal matters and in one's choice of career. It is full of life force and vitality and greatly assists the body to heal itself by its support of tissue regeneration and its ability as an evolved mineral healer.

Grounding and stimulating, it enhances life force and chi, renewing energy and overcoming lethargy. Optimism and motivation is increased. Carnelian stimulates and inspires personal power and physical energy, giving courage and strength.

Carnelian can aid confidence, boldness and assertiveness so is also popular with actors as it enhances dramatic abilities. It has sometimes been called the "actor's stone". It adds more inspiration and passion to your mind and your life. It assists memory, and has been known to aid in the recall of past lives. Carnelian works on the mental level by improving analytical abilities and also aids to clarify perception.

Thinking precision is improved. Concentration is sharpened as mental lethargy is dispersed. Negative conditionings can be overcome with this stone and it assists to get to the bottom of one's motivations and agendas. Together with a greater awareness and acceptance of one's own feelings.

It is said to be able to assist one in finding the right mate and there is an increase in self trust. Steadfastness is encouraged, and emotional negativity is replaced with a new love of life.

It is also a stone of protection in general and can protect in particular from anger, jealousy and fear.

Carnelian can help ease or remove sorrows. It also helps stabilise energies in the home.

Carnelian is associated with the root and sacral Chakras. The heart Chakra can be supported and Carnelian can also strengthen all of the meridians and associated nadis. The alignment between the etheric and physical bodies is improved.

Carnelian also helps people who meditate to ground better afterwards.

Physically, carnelian has been used to heal open sores, rejuvenate tissues and cells, rheumatism, kidney stones and other kidney problems, gall stones, colds, pollen allergies, and neuralgia. It is recognised as assisting in the areas of fertility and potency and libido.

Carnelian is one of the few stones that does not need cleaning, you can keep in with other stones to keep them fresh and clean. However, I still regularly I rinse mine off occasionally and also re-charge them so they can remain fresh and happy in their work

Keywords for Carnelian are: Vitality, Protection, Motivation.

16. Cerussite

Cerussite has a number of formations, and it often appears as a clumping or group of spindles or fine crystalline strands set in various directions, almost as though they are magnetized in the middle and this is what holds them all together. They can also appear as chunkier crystals with normal crystal points or tabular-type points and levels. Sometimes they are found growing together on another crystal or rock matrix.

They can look extraordinary when they appear as natural star formations. Colours can vary from clear or misty white to creams or browns.

Cerussite is softer than diamond and so harder to facet, though it lends itself beautifully to gems with Star-Facets. It has a high lead content, and is highly toxic so should have limited handling.

When the Cerussite is formed in a star-shape or is clumped with record-keeper markings, they are excellent for use in attuning to higher wisdom and for working with karmic issues and purpose. Its energies help one to feel more "at home" wherever they are, and in particular to help the soul to feel more comfortable on Planet Earth if it feels "homesick" or alienated in any way. It is perfect for past life exploration, particularly if these were not on Earth. Releasing the past is a gift with this crystal.

Cerussite is also beneficial for travel of any kind and can assist in reducing jet-lag. It is easier to adjust to other cultures and to make temporary adjustments or compromises when inner resistance is strong.

Its ability to work with difficulties and obstacles in a practical and understanding way is unique. Cerussite allows one to easily adapt to various situations and to changes when needed by helping one to know that the changes are only transient.

Cerussite also provides one with the strength to manage one's composure with the conditions of the current reality.

It is also said to facilitate access to connections with other planetary beings, while allowing one to remember other worlds and other times, including those who have been parts of their past lives. This is important in order to identify any that are holding one back in this present life.

Cerussite's vibration can bring amazing change into one's life and is especially beneficial if you desire to make changes in your ordinary day-to-day life, and in particular to find a new life path or different career... especially one of a spiritual nature.

It is a very grounding crystal and has the ability to help one to ground to the "here and now".

It also enables greater contact and access with one's higher self, assisting with translating higher concepts into everyday language and perceptions.

It supports psychic-ness, aiding psychic ability with greater clarity. Cerussite can also show us what we can and what we cannot change.

Physically, Cerussite helps support and align the network of the nervous system to provide for free flow of energy as well as better grounding.

The meaning of Cerussite's name relates an ancient Latin word 'Cerussa' meaning "white lead".

Note: Because of its possible toxicity, never attempt to make up your own gem elixir with this stone unless you know exactly what you are doing.

Keywords for Cerussite: Understanding Obstacles, Stress Relief, Change.

17. Chevron Amethyst

Chevron Amethyst is a combination of Amethyst and White Quartz, mixed together in a V-striped or banded pattern. It is sometimes called Banded Amethyst and it can appear as though there are a series of chevron bands within the crystal.

Amethyst has long been known as the master of ceremonies when it comes to spirituality. The powerful protection it brings creating a bubble around the carrier, warding off psychic attacks and negative energy.

It is also seen as the sobering stone. In some crystal healing circles Amethyst is also known as a "Master Healing Crystal". Amethyst clears and purifies assisting with stress and tension, it soothes and calms the mind, raises the spirit and protects from negative vibrations.

It is known to provide protection and balance during transition periods. It also reduces the feeling of being victimized, giving one a spiritual perspective on life's circumstances.

Chevron Amethyst combines the strengthening and enhancing qualities of Quartz with the stress relieving qualities of Amethyst. Together these minerals create the Chevron Amethyst, which is noted in metaphysics to enhance peace of mind, relaxation and self-discovery. This symbiotic combination of minerals lends itself to a wonderfully spiritual stone, which is great for gently removing the veils that obscure some of the hidden meanings in life.

Chevron Amethyst has all the healing properties of Amethyst and also a few additional qualities. The banded variety is excellent for working with and stimulating the third eye Chakra.

It can enhance intuition and is a powerful stone for dissipating and repelling negativity. It has a cleansing effect on the aura.

Chevron amethyst is said to bring courage and inner strength. The stone is said in mystical lore to lessen any resistance to helping oneself, particularly as concerns self-awareness. It also is said to diminish addictive tendencies and assists in recovery from addictions.

Note that healing crystal meanings are spiritual supports to healing and are not prescriptions or healthcare information. Chevron amethyst is associated with the third eye (brow) or crown Chakra. In addition to its own qualities it also has meanings of amethyst and quartz.

Chevron Amethyst is one of the best stones to work with the Third-Eye, enhancing both intuition and physical vision on all planes of existence. The Chevron Amethyst helps peel off old karmic patterns to promote self-love and the ability to get along with others especially with one's Soul Mate or family members.

One can use Chevron Amethyst to help remove resistance to change, and to dissipate and repel negativity of all kinds.

Chevron Amethyst creates a strong healing field around the user, and as such, is a good choice to cleanse the aura and to enhance the immune system.

Crystal healers work with Chevron Amethyst for its psychic energies and for its ability to clear and strengthen the aura. Chevron Amethyst can amplify energies needed for manifestation and works well in grid work. Chevron Amethyst is also said to deepen the meditative state, enhancing the quality and frequency of visions and inspiration from higher realms.

Keywords for Chevron Amethyst are: "Master Healer", Protection, Peace of Mind, Self-awareness, Inner Strength.

18. Citrine

The color of Citrine is usually a pale golden yellow, but can be found in darker shades as well, and can be either transparent or semi-transparent. Its colours can be so closely related to the Sun that it seems to bring a sense of joy, happiness and abundance.

Citrine is known as the "success stone" because it promotes success, prosperity, and abundance. It particularly promotes success in business, earning it another nickname, "merchant's stone", and is said to bring business if put in the cashbox of a shop or carried. Citrine is a stone of good fortune, although it brings good fortune in sometimes unexpected ways. It is a stone of manifestation, helping manifest abundance in many ways. Along with prosperity and good fortune, Citrine imparts generosity, to share the wealth, so to speak.

Citrine has Electromagnetic properties and is able to cleanse other crystals.

Citrine dissipates negative energies of all kinds. It also does not absorb any negative energies from its surroundings, and thus never needs energetic clearing. Citrine can be used to clear unwanted energies from the environment. Family issues caused by negative energies can also be resolved and cleared with Citrine. Since Citrine eliminates negative energies, it helps generate stability in all areas.

In the mental area, Citrine enhances mental clarity, confidence, and will power. It also increases creativity and promotes honesty. The mental body are harmonized with higher spiritual laws, providing an increased access to divine truth and intelligence. Citrine is excellent for amplifying the qualities of concentration, centering, and a balanced rational mind. Its ability to cleanse and clear negative energies also has the effect of bringing clarity to a situation as well as to one's thoughts concerning it.

Emotionally, Citrine relieves depression, self-doubt, anger, and irrational mood swings. Citrine is a stone that brings happiness and cheer to one who carries or wears it. It also reduces self-destructive tendencies.

Citrine helps eliminate fears caused by others' ideas and suggestions. It can help one overcome emotional traumas and grief. Sensuality and sexuality can also be heightened by Citrine.

In the psychic and spiritual realms, Citrine is good for general psychic awareness and spiritual development. Citrine clears the aura of negative energies and influences. It is also very useful for meditation. Citrine is a stone of protection, removing or deflecting negative energies of all kinds. It is also excellent for dream recall and dream work.

Physically, Citrine is beneficial for the digestion, stomach, eliminating nightmares and other sleep disturbances, thyroid, general health, heart, kidney, liver, muscles, strength, endocrine system, circulatory system, tissue regeneration, urinary system, immune system, fibromyalgia. Citrine is also good for removing toxins, and overcoming addictions.

Citrine is associated with the Solar Plexus Chakra.

It can be used in healing not only to initiate healing directly but also to support other healing crystals with its ability to cleanse and clear energies as the healing progresses.

Citrine is known as a "success" stone as it promotes success and abundance, especially in business and commerce. Citrine enhances mental clarity, confidence, happiness and will power. It can also bring good fortune in sometimes unexpected ways.

Citrine can alleviate depression and self-doubt, and helps diminish irrational mood swings due to its effect of mental clarity. It can aid the digestion and eliminate nightmares that disturb one's sleep.

Keywords for Citrine are: "Success Stone", "Merchant's Stone", Abundance.

19. Clear Quartz Crystal

Clear Quartz is a power stone that harmonises and balances. It enhances energy and thoughts, and purifies the spiritual, mental, and physical.

Historically this crystal has been used to counter black magic, to perform diagnostic healing, and to communicate with spirits and other worlds.

Clear quartz is associated with the crown Chakra, but also works well on all Chakras.

There is much more about Clear Quartz in the section on Quartz Crystal Functions.

20. Danburite

Danburite is often transparent or translucent though it can also be cloudy. Its colours vary from being colourless or of the palest pink, light pink, champagne or yellow to brownish. It feels very light to the touch, and in its rough form is usually as crystal points with lengthwise striations.

Danburite is known for its pure and high vibration, and it is indeed one of the highest vibration minerals currently found and is known to "Connect the Heart of the Mind with the Mind of the Heart".

To me it feels like a stone of joy, light and peace. It is a clear crystal in that it feels clear and it brings truth, honesty and illumination. It is said to bring a smile to the heart and open receptivity to both mind and spirit.

It is a highly spiritual crystal and is often sought after for its metaphysical properties. Danburite is a powerful heart Chakra stone, relieving emotional pain and increasing acceptance of one's self and of others. Danburite is said to help you "let your light shine". The pure Love Energy of Danburite is extremely comforting and brings serenity and peace.

Danburite powerfully radiates bright, pure, white light, filling the body, mind, and spirit as well as one's relationships with loving light. Its energy is very soothing and comforting. It is thought to encourage the release of anxiety, fear and grief and to bring feelings of serenity, calm and patience. It has the ability to bring light to old festering wounds and to encourage emotional healing.

It is an Excellent healing tool as it strengthens the mind and nervous system, bringing in greater life force and awareness. It also brings a lovely soothing energy.

Gentle yet powerful Danburite also works with the Third Eye and Crown Chakras. Danburite stimulates the Higher Chakras, connecting the Heart to these Higher Chakras, and aids in communication with Angels and Guides.

Danburite is a good stone to have around during times of extreme change, and eases the transition of those leaving the physical human form. It is an excellent healing stone. Danburite can help heal old deep wounds, as well as support work around clearing past karma by clarifying the associated lessons.

Used in healing, Danburite will enhance the functionality of all the Chakras. It also has the ability to amplify the properties and effects of other stones.

It is an excellent healing crystal for it can gently open and release existing energy blockages, bringing healing on all levels. It is very healing during times of dramatic change.

It can assist to ease the transition of those challenged or preparing to move on from the physical human form, so is a good bedside companion for those dying as it can also bring peace to the soul and mind.

Danburite is a powerful heart Chakra stone and is said to assist in releasing emotional blockages whilst increasing acceptance of one's self and of others. It has the ability to encourage emotional healing, bringing light to old festering wounds, whilst also bringing in serenity, calm and patience.

Danburite is also helpful in strengthening clarity and perceptiveness. It also lessens issues of self-pride as well as diminishing blockages.

Its energy is said to activate both the higher levels of consciousness and the academic mind.

It is a lovely meditation stone as it helps to build a bridge to the spiritual and encourages one to access inner guidance, whilst also being able to activate both the intellect and the academic mind and higher levels of consciousness which allows one to link in to the spiritual and angelic realms. Danburite encourages one to "let your light shine".

Keywords for Danburite: Connecting Mind and Heart, Release Energy Blockages, Healing, Compassion.

21. Dendritic Agate

Dendritic Agates are usually colorless, white, or gray, and have tree- or fern-like inclusions of iron or manganese, called dendrites. The less common variety are green Tree Agates with white dendrites. Usually Agate is banded, but not so with this variety.

The name Dendritic is derived from the Greek word meaning tree-like. The dendrites can make pretty and interesting fern-like designs within the agate, often creating unique cameo pictures that lend well to adornment as jewelry. Often the shapes within represent plants, and sometimes animals. The minerals within give extra strength and fortitude to the crystal, whilst the randomness of the patterns provides a uniqueness to confirm the uniqueness of the individual.

Historically, Agate has been discovered with the ancient artifacts of Neolithic people, and was thought to be used as healing amulets and ornamentation dating back to Babylon. Its uses appear to have continued through the ancient Greek and Egyptian civilizations, and spread throughout Africa and the Middle East into Russia. Agate sparked a world renowned stonecutting and polishing industry in Germany that flourished from the 15th to the 19th century, and exists today.

Metaphysically, Agate has a lower intensity and vibrates to a slower frequency than other stones, but is highly regarded as a stabilizing and strengthening influence. It is a gentle yet persistent stress soother.

Dendritic Agate assists in overcoming emotional boundary violations and to offset the accompanying emotional strain.

It can help heal the pain caused by an unhappy childhood or the hurtful effects of a divorce and is useful for any kind of trauma.

Agate has the power to overcome negativity and bitterness of the heart. By its ability to heal anger it can foster love. And is able to lend the courage to start over.

Like all agates, it has the ability to stabilize the aura, eliminating and transforming negative energies. Its cleansing effect is powerful at can work all levels.

Dendritic Agate stimulates the Base or Root Chakra which assists to support the foundation of physical and spiritual energy for the body. When the Base Chakra is in balance, the physical body gains strength and stamina, and spiritual energy is rekindled in the form of a sense of security and of one's own power. This often leads to independence and spontaneous leadership.

Dendritic Agate is known as the "Stone of Plentitude". It has the ability to bring abundance and fullness to all areas of life, from business to agricultural endeavors.

It has been associated with the ancient Greek dryads, woodland and tree spirits, and an ancient practice was to bury some in the fields at the time of sowing to insure a good harvest.

It has a strong connection to the plant kingdom and deepens our own connection to the Earth and our place in the Universe.

It resonates to deep peace, assisting in supporting the nervous system and anything that appears to branch out, such as blood vessels and nerves.

Dendritic Agate encourages perseverance and patience, and promotes a peaceful inner and outer environment. It allows one to grow spiritually whilst still remaining connected with ones roots, and it aligns the Chakras enabling integration with one's higher consciousness.

Green Dendritic Agates are considered to be "growth crystals" and as such are powerful conduits of the earth's Life Force and cycle of birth and development.

It symbolizes creation and the power of nature's constant renewal. They are strongly connected to nurturing new ventures or fledgling family relationships.

Lighter Green crystals are considered to promote spiritual growth and renewed commitment to a higher purpose.

White or Silver Dendritic Agate: White is the color of cleanliness, purity, unity and innocence, and a symbol of the timeless, natural reflective powers of the moon's white rays. It heralds the color of natural cycles, birth, and regeneration, and supports the feminine, seen as the Goddess in many cultures.

As the moonlight lightens the dark world of night, these white talismans speak of the spiritual world that is sensed but not seen. They may well act as guides to higher understanding and knowledge.

Keywords: "Stone of Plenitude", Stimulates Healers.

22. Dumortierite (Blue quartz)

Dumortierite is known as a blue quartz crystal, though Dumortierite itself is the blue within the crystal and most Dumortierite crystals are actually Dumortierite mixed with quartz, this is why some pieces are very dark blue (more Dumortierite) and others are pale blue (more quartz).

It is generally opaque, but there are some gem quality pieces that polish up as clear gems.

Quartz is extremely powerful as an energy storer and transmitter, so combining it in this way with the energy of blue aids greatly in calming the mind, bringing peace and assuaging fear.

It is excellent for reducing emotional tension and bringing order into one's sphere as well as enhancing one's organisational abilities, self-discipline and orderliness.

Some believe this is because it effectively balances the Throat Chakra and enhances communication between the lower Chakras and the higher Chakras – thus aligning the physical with the mental and spiritual. Difficulties through having a scattered mind are greatly reduced and discipline and courage to order and organize are greatly enhanced. A sense of order is brought to all things, and it greatly emphasizes increased energy and boosts creative expression and self expression.

Blue quartz helps reduce emotional tension and is excellent for peaceful mindfulness or meditation. It brings compassion for the processes in life as well as for the self.

One is also encouraged to see and accept reality, and to react to it in an intelligent manner on one's own behalf.

Dumortierite is said to promote a positive attitude to life and to help one to stay 'young at heart'.

It is also said to increase assertiveness and self-confidence encouraging you to speak out when you feel you are being treated unfairly. Another gift is its ability to help to calm and focus the mind in traumatic situations, thus allowing easy access to the tools required to cope with the crisis.

Physically, it helps to purify the bloodstream and to strengthen the immune system.

It is a brilliant stone for success and business with its ability to focus the mind and to create better organising as well as to create opportunities to do things better.

Because of its blue element capacity, Dumortierite is wonderful for the Throat Chakra. This makes it apt as a stone of communication and it can greatly stimulate the verbalization of ideas and the ability to get them across to others more easily.

Dumortierite is also a stone of support, as it helps with those who may feel less than confident in thought and idea. It also assists in staying true and in standing up for one's self.

It is also a perfect choice for families. Dumortierite helps to reduce excitability and stubbornness for children. For parents, it is an excellent stone for calm and patience.

Dumortierite is a very spiritual stone and it is believed to facilitate communication with one's angels and spirit guides.

It also allows one to more easily see the good where it exists in the people who are around you. Because Blue Quartz has this spiritual aspect to it, it aids in the understanding of one's spiritual nature.

It also inspires hope in healing. Dumortierite offers soothing vibrations that encourages patience with the natural order of the Universe.

This action can help one to remain in a state of allowing, accepting that the process of manifestation may work more slowly at times.

Dumortierite also promotes an understanding of karma and forgiveness, especially self-forgiveness.

Keywords for Dumortierite are: Travel Stress, Patience, Support, Self-Expression, Order, Peace.

23. Fire Agate

Agates are from the Chalcedony family and are usually formed from microscopic crystals of quartz laid down in bands. All agates are very grounding stones and because they work slowly yet surely are very stabilizing crystals. They often appear layered and can have a waxy feel to them yet this banding allows the revealing of hidden information as and when one is ready to deal with it.

Fire Agate can manifest as twisted bands of pearlised matter or with bubbles of these rainbow- type pearls along its surface. However they appear, there is always a kind of fire and glow to them.

The supportive energies of Agates can foster love, abundance, wealth, good luck, longevity. They also allow the space to nurture self and other acceptance, increase courage and they provide protection.

Other gifts are the ability to support the being with greater balance and harmony, and to free one's feelings of generosity, both towards the self and towards others.

It also brings with it the ability to gain and gather strength, which engenders more security in the self and in life. Agates are also very calming and soothing to the emotions. Agate supports and stabilizes the aura, so is good for cleansing and clearing it as well as supporting the body's subtle energies.

This family of stones allows for healing of emotional ill-ease, gifting a greater acceptance of love and courage to start again.

One can gain a greater sense and appreciation of nature with this stone. Agates are considered very powerful stones and this is amplified in Fire Agate.

Fire Agate takes its name from the combination of swirling bands of colours of fire that bring a luminescent to the exposed bands. It is almost as though someone has dropped whirls of pearlised deep reds and oranges into the crystal that catch the light and then sealed it with clear plastic.

The Fire Agate expands further on the ability to not only calm but also to bring greater acceptance and safety as it grounds with a greater connection to the earth. It is a stone that brings great courage, supports this courage with strength and energises one towards one's true path. It also is highly protective which supports one's spiritual journey and process. Fire Agate has the ability to balance both active and receptive energies, both male and female aspects of the being.

Even though it is so fortifying, it also has the ability to induce a sense of calm and a feeling of relaxation. It helps to take the edge of difficult or upsetting experiences. When used with other crystals or other healing modalities it is said to expand the effect and benefits.

It has been known to relieve fear and even to halt gossip, reflecting any harm back to its original source and it has been claimed that it is able to effectively build a protective shield around the body, which deflects ill-wishing and reflecting it back.

Fire Agate is an excellent stone to use before meditating. It is believed to instill courage and spiritual fortitude, to reduce fear and to encourage feelings of security and safety. It also helps one to examine and deal with problems in a calm and safe manner.

In addition it is said to stimulate energy and life force and to increase sexual vitality.

Some have claimed it is excellent to use with Color Therapy.

Fire Agates main keywords are: "Spiritual Flame of Perfection", Energising, Protection, Courage.

24. Hematite

Hematite is an interesting stone. It is a dark silvery black with a very metallic feel to it. It was regarded by the ancients as the "Stone of the Warrior". Being comprised of iron oxide it can also be a steel grey to iron black in color. This silver-grey mineral is actually an iron ore comprised of iron oxide.

It is one of the most grounding of all stones and resonates to the Base or Root Chakra.

Hematite grounds excess and chaotic energy and condenses scattered-ness. You can sometimes find sets of two toggle shaped Hematites that together demonstrate their magnetic quality by showing both attraction and repulsion qualities.

Hematite is good at grounding out excess energy and acting as a stabilising force. It is known to ground the ultra sensitive, and even a simple finger ring of Hematite can assist in bringing the psychic or sensitive back into their body again after intense energy work, meditation or from being disconnected from their physical selves.

Hematite is also known as a "stone for the mind". It assists with mental organisation and is very grounding and calming. Hematite helps with original thought, logical thinking, and mathematics. Hematite assists to transform fuzziness into mental clarity, improving concentration, memory, and practicality as well as helping with study and mental tasks such as bookkeeping or detail work. . Confidence is increased and will power is improved. The Ancient Egyptians used Hematite to calm hysteria and anxiety.

Emotionally, Hematite helps us maintain a state of compassionate detachment while witnessing an intense emotional experience in another, and helps us to contain our own emotional experiences in a responsible way. It is a protective stone that also helps bolster low self-esteem. It decreases negativity and can help balance the body, mind and spirit.

It strengthens one's energetic boundaries in the emotional body and so promotes emotional independence rather than codependency. The iron in this stone has a strong effect on the blood.

For feelings of defenselessness it helps one to adapt to being in a physical body. Because of its strength and vitality qualities, it supports firmness, strength, dedication, attraction and achievement. It is also mentally calming as it balances energy.

It can assist in grounding spiritual energy with the Earth Star Chakra and the Fourth Earthing Chakra as well as providing spiritual protection.

Physically it has been used to keep the body cool, to decrease blood disorders, nervous problems and insomnia, as well as align the spine and mend broken bones. It is excellent for stress relief. It has been used in supporting the kidney's blood-cleansing function and is said to help in tissue regeneration.

Hematite helps the body and being to regroup after jet lag, and periods of serious stress. It also aids the body to recover after experiencing birth or anaesthesia.

Keywords for Hematite are "Stone of the Warrior", "Stone for the Mind", Magnetic, Vitality, Protection.

25. Labradorite

Labradorite is such an initially deceptive stone. At first glance it can look dull and appear to have grey or black veins and stripes throughout. Then when the light hits its surface it suddenly reveals hidden lights that make it glow with an iridescent sheen, revealing amazing depths and flashes of deep blues and peacock greens. It commonly has blue to golden green flashes when viewed at certain angles, and appears metallic iridescent.

Labradorite is often referred to as the "Stone of Destiny" as it is believed to help to find one's true path in life. Labradorite has sometimes been referred to as Spectrolite and was considered by mystics to be a stone of transformation.

Labradorite dissolves illusions and true intentions are seen with much more clarity with its use. It strengthens the Aura and is hugely protective against negative energies, keeping you clean and clear energetically. Labradorite is also said to promote wisdom, understanding and patience and to help banish fears and insecurities. It is said to clear, balance and protect the aura. In addition it is believed to protect and cushion the aura by helping to deflect unwanted energies. Labradorite is said to increase intuition, psychic development, esoteric wisdom, help with subconscious issues, and provide mental illumination.

The iridescent energies bathe and nourish the entire energy system with full spectrum light which represents the light of the universe bringing illumination.

Labradorite can temper the negative side of one's personality, balancing the traits and actions that may rob one's energy and may produce depression or shame. It can also assist in reducing anti-social, reckless or impulsive behavior in children, teenagers and adults who are easily led into trouble by others. This makes it a good stone for childhood issues. Besides that, it is also thought to aid in detoxifying the effects of tobacco, alcohol, and to a lesser degree, hard drugs.

For those whose relationships rarely meet expectations and for tension arising from frustration, Labradorite renews and refreshes one's perspective, assisting one to again glimpse the magnificent in the mundane, and the divine in the ordinary. This extraordinary stone encourages intuition, inspiration, mental activity and opens the consciousness.

Labradorite calms an overactive mind and energizes the imagination, bringing in new ideas. It supports Intuition, and aids in balancing the subconscious. It is a wonderful tool for returning joy and spontaneity back to one's life. It helps eliminate the emotional drain of daily routine or being weighed down by responsibility, and awakens a sense of adventure and change.

Labradorite is also the most powerful protector of the mineral kingdom, creating a shielding force throughout the aura and strengthening natural energies from within. It protects against the negativity and misfortunes of this world, and provides safe exploration into alternate levels of consciousness and in facilitating visionary experiences from the past or the future. It can help to develop the hands' sensitivity, making it useful for physiotherapists and all who use the power of touch to heal.

As a workplace stone Labradorite can help to bring out the best in people which assists in making work life more congenial. It can also encourage courtesy and attention toward the customer, and assist casual staff to become more involved in a company.

In healing Labradorite is believed to relieve stress and menstrual tension, fend off colds, lower blood pressure and regulate metabolism. Stress and anxiety is reduced, quite possibly due to its ability to increase the energy of self-confidence.

Keywords for Labradorite are: "Stone of Destiny", Protection, Childhood Issues, Relationships, Intuition.

26. Lapis Lazuli

It is a very attractive stone of deep rich blues that appears to be veined and flecked with gold and sometimes silver or mica.

Its name has been traced to the Persian 'Lazhuward' – "blue", and the Latin 'Lapis' – "stone". Formed by layers of many minerals, it looks like the beautiful deep blue is scattered and mixed with flecks of gold, silver, white and grey. Lapis Lazuli has been around since the beginning of man's history, and was plentiful in the days of the Pharaohs of Ancient Egypt.

Its celestial blue is connected to the blue of the heavens, as well as the ultramarine blue of the seas. It has been used for gems and jewellery, eye shadow adornment, and for its ultramarine dye properties, as well as for its symbolical connections. Painters have used it to capture a certain kind of richness in their paintings.

Since ancient times, there have been many powers attributed to Lapis including wisdom, spiritual growth, psychic ability, protection, potential, memory, meditation and truth. Lapis is a deep balancer, healing chest and throat areas and helpful for easing stress and trauma from whole body.

The rich blues indicate its connection with the Throat and the Third Eye Chakras, and its ability to enhance creative expression and knowledge. It can also amplify the ability to hear information from physical and nonphysical sources and it helps clear confusion between hearing and knowing. It can increase psychic abilities and will assist to enhance the third eye capacity. It is claimed to be able to guide in the direction of mental and spiritual purity.

Lapis Lazuli is reputed to assist with the intellect and learning, enhancing these abilities, and stimulating the desire for knowledge, truth and understanding. It aids and encourages honesty of the spirit, and therefore works toward harmony in relationships, and with all forms of deep communication.

Lapis encourages and enhances courage, creative expression, fidelity, higher self, healing, illumination, joy, love, mental clarity, opens Chakras, psychic abilities, protection, psychism, spirit guides, strength, virility, vitality. This indicates its comprehensive healing and supporting abilities. And it is a good stone for protection from evil intent.

Beneficial to the respiratory system, especially the throat and lungs, the cleansing organs, and the nervous system, Lapis is a good stone for blood purification and for boosting the immune system. It is a powerful thought-amplifier and is helpful in aligning all the elements of the body and mind. When wearing as jewelry it helps to wear it as close to the throat as possible or at least above the diaphragm so that the energy of the wearer is drawn upward.

The dark blue of Lapis enhances our self-respect. The crystal can be a catalyst for higher awareness, aiding us in learning of our humanity, discretion, and honor. It can teach us sensitivity to the needs of others, bringing more tenderness in our interactions, and enhancing our understanding of personal evolution to further our development. For those working with Past Live Regressions or self journeying, it can assist in recovering lifetimes in ancient civilizations – Sumeria, Egypt, India, Peru, Atlantis – and help is regain lost knowledge from these times.

Lapis Lazuli, with its beautiful blue, the original colour of the feminine (not the current pink associated with the female aspect) has been associated with several Goddesses. Inanna, the Sumerian Goddess of the Underworld has been associated with journeying carrying her Lapis Lazuli rods, to measure the time and length of a person's life. Nuit or Nut, the Egyptian Goddess of Heaven and Sky, swallows the sun each evening, giving birth to it again each morning and she known as the protector and mother of life on Earth. Hera, Greek Goddess of Marriage, and Queen of all Gods and Goddesses on Mt Olympus, was the source of inspiration for wives and lovers, encouraging one standing up for what is right. Danu, the Celtic River Goddess has been connected with Lapis as has Venus, the Roman Goddess of Love, though in the Greek, she was also known as Aphrodite.

This crystal can assist with manifestation through its ability to support the mental and emotional processes, and to encourage wisdom. This supports the manifesting process which usually begins with the mind and imagination first (how else could we make something happen without thinking of it first?) is easier - and Lapis can then further help with its energy to support bringing more organisation and order into our minds and lives. Because Lapis Lazuli lessens confusion and aids concentration, as well as enhancing creativity this aids the mental clarity necessary to hold the thought and the energy necessary to truly manifest.

Note of caution: Sometimes Howlite has been dyed a similar blue and can at first glance look like Lapis, so look for the beautiful starry specks and the "depth" underneath the surface of the various blue colours within the stone, almost as if it has been 'coated'. Howlite appears more one-dimensional or opaque. Effective and pretty as Howlite is, it cannot replicate the beauty and energy of true Lapis.

Keywords for Lapis Lazuli are Communication, Protection, Wisdom.

27. Lepidolite

Lepidolite is usually found in colours of Pink, purple, rose-red, violet-gray, but also yellowish, white and colourless. It is more commonly recognized in soft lavender or lilac to soft pink that is usually dull, sparkly or a combination of both.

Lepidolite is a lithium-mica, and this mica often gives it a muted sparkly appearance. Because it is so high in lithium it was originally mined for this mineral. It feels smooth to the touch.

Lepidolite has extremely high vibrations and is known as a "Stone of Transition". It is particularly good for assisting in the restructuring and reorganization of old patterns, and so helps to overcome dependencies.

It is believed to work very effectively on the brain's pain centers helping to alleviate drug addiction and bipolar disorder whilst helping to stabilize mood swings.

Lepidolite is a stone of calm, trust, and acceptance and it has a strong calming and relaxing effect.

It brings hope and as a stone of transformation it helps one get through transitions with trust that everything will ultimately turn out for the best. It engenders and enhances self-love, patience, and optimism, imparting calmness. When combined with Rubellite (Pink Tourmaline) it is an extraordinarily powerful agent for calming and healing, especially in the emotional areas.

It works upon the nervous system and the brain and is particularly useful for alleviating stress of any sort. It is particularly effective for emotional balance, engendering calm and is beneficial where there is depression or past trauma including PTSD (Post Traumatic Stress Disorder).

It is an excellent emotional healer, and is perfect for alleviating anxiety, manic-depression, despondency, anger, panic attacks, and addictions. Gently eases intensity of feelings, stress, mood swings, self-criticism and worrying.

Lepidolite gently brings hope, relief and gentleness, encouraging self-love, patience, and self-forgiveness. This also works to assist better sleep, as well as greater mental and emotional balance and a greater sense of well-being.

It reduces obsessive thinking and confusion and is said to stimulate the intellect and to help one to focus on what is important.

Physically, Lepidolite is said to be helpful for healing of glands, immune system, skin, nails, hair, DNA, enzyme balance, addiction and alcoholism recovery, childbirth, and general healing.

Placed under the pillow, or by the side of the bed, Lepidolite is said to help overcome insomnia.

Lepidolite is said to be powerful in overcoming all kinds of emotional or mental dependency, assisting in the release of addictions, including eating disorders such as bulimia, anorexia and over-eating.

Placed directly on the body Lepidolite is said to ease joint problems, to numb sciatica, to relieve allergies and to strengthen the immune system.

Psychically, Lepidolite has been used for dream-work or rebirthing. It is also good for dream recall.

Lepidolite activates the Throat, Heart, Brow and Crown Chakras bringing cosmic awareness and aiding deep meditation by clearing unwanted debris from the mind.

Lepidolite is also a protective stone that brings success in business or career.

Lepidolite keywords include: Mood Enhancer, Balance, Awareness, Transition and Transformation.

28. Morganite (Pink Beryl)

Morganite is the pale pink variety of the Beryl family, as is Aquamarine. It can range from very pale pink, soft pink, violet-pink, pale salmon and peach pink and is a very gentle stone. It can manifest as totally transparent or as cloudy, and its gentleness supports all relationships. The shades of pink reflect the Light of the heart and love, and help stimulate the heart and the Heart Chakra in a timely and gently nurturing manner. This is a Crystal of Divine Love.

It is said to have the ability to both attract, to hold and to maintain romantic love and it supports the wearer through its willingness to only work at the rate that the heart is ready to activate. Morganite is claimed to be a remarkable crystal for attracting one's soul-mate or deepening a current relationship.

Because it is also a heart opener like Rose Quartz it has a powerful impact on the heart, but its actions are always nurturing and gentle, and it eases and cleanses old emotional traumas and wounds with care. It is perfect for each user as it provides support to the nervous system and melts resistance to healing the heart and its associated pains and past issues in a gentle manner.

With its gentle and soothing pink energy, Morganite attunes to the heart and the Heart Chakra. It cleanses the emotional body of stress and anxiety, and of old wounds and hidden traumas.

It can rekindle or introduce lightness within the spirit, as if a burden has been lifted. Its ability to bring in the frequency of Divine compassion inspires a greater awareness that life's suffering or pain might have served a higher purpose in one's spiritual growth, and may well have been a catalyst for moving forward in peace and confidence.

Morganite encourages you to have loving thoughts and actions, reducing stress and helping you to appreciate and enjoy your life Stress relief,

Morganite with its clear, peach-pink innocence embodies the first pale rays of sunrise that swells the heart and warms the soul, releasing a sense of smallness in a vast universe and opening to the overwhelming presence of a Higher power.

Morganite is thought to help you become aware of ignored, unfulfilled needs and to aid you in recognising and releasing unexpressed feelings and emotions. It brings healing, compassion, assurance and promise.

Morganite can encourage fair and just treatment of others, especially those with mental or emotional problems or physical illnesses that may possibly make them hostile to others. It is an ideal crystal for realizing the equality in all relationships, and in developing effective but loving communication and expression.

This stone brings Emotional Balance and assists one to overcome fear, resentment and anger. It acts to help one to recognise unfulfilled emotional needs and hidden or buried feelings which have gone unexpressed or get in the way of love. It can also gently reveal defense mechanisms that are fear-based and that have made meaningful relationships difficult, which may have resulted in creating resistance to healing or to love and self transformation.

Morganite stabilizes the emotional field, activating and energizing loving thoughts and actions, and brings in the energy of wisdom and a calmness of mind. It greatly increases the ability to accept loving words and actions from others, and can assist one to release the old stories and attachment to old relationships that have ended badly or that have needed further resolution.

Resolving these then encourages one to move forward with a renewed purpose and an open heart again. It encourages loving thoughts and actions, consideration and responsibility, and being receptive to love from others.

Because of its connection to Divine energies, may also be used for peace and acceptance when facing grief or deep loss

Keywords for Morganite include: Divine Love, Spiritual Lovingness, Emotional Balance and Equality.

29. Onyx

Onyx is more often associated with its black variety, though it also comes in other colours and white. It is usually polished and can also be banded or may appear marble-like.

Black Onyx is an excellent stone to have around during times of mental or physical stress. It provides strength and support during difficult circumstances, assisting to bring soothing to alleviate fears and worries. One tends to feel more comfortable within the self and in one's surroundings. It assists with facing and solving challenges, stabilizing and balancing emotions.

Black Onyx aids the development of emotional and physical strength and stamina, especially when support is needed during times of stress, confusion or grief. It fosters wise decision making, and because of its abilities as a powerful protection stone, Black Onyx absorbs and transforms negative energy, and helps to prevent the drain of one's own personal energy.

Not only does it help to ground one's energies and activities, it encourages intuition and awareness of inner guidance. Black Onyx encourages happiness and good fortune. It is a strength-giving stone and can provide support for self-discipline issues too.

Because Black Onyx is useful in healing physical memories, it assists in moving past and healing old wounds or past life issues.

It also assists to ground romantic love into reality.

Black Onyx also assists to support the emotions and brings stamina when faced with a bereavement.

Black Onyx is said to promote self-control helping the wearer to keep excessive emotions and passions under control.

Onyx is associated primarily with the root Chakra. It assists with challenges in life, especially those caused by a drain of energy. It prevents the draining away of personal energy and can be used for protection from such.

It also helps with grounding and controlling or eliminating excess or unwanted energies. It prevents the draining away of personal energy and can be used for protection from such. It also helps with grounding and controlling or eliminating excess or unwanted energies.

An Onyx can retain memory of the physical occurrences surrounding a person, so is therefore a strong stone to use in psychometry because of this ability to tell the story of the wearer.

Onyx is a strength-giving stone. It is an excellent stone for athletes or people under extreme mental and emotional stress. It brings balance to mind or body as well as strength of mind. It is also a good stone for those who are flighty by nature.

Onyx is a strengthening stone that can help you approach a lesson or task with greater self- confidence. Said to be good for the teeth and bones.

For sensitive types, it is often recommended that Onyx be used with Pearl or Diamond to enhance and make the most of the heavy grounding and strengthening effects in a more gentle way.

Black onyx and red onyx are associated with the base (root, first) Chakra. It has also been used for wound healing and childbirth.

White onyx is associated with linking the base and crown Chakras to have balanced energy throughout the Chakra system.

Keywords for Onyx are Grounding, Stress Support, Strength-Giving, Self-Control, Protection.

30. Pink ManganoCalcite (Pink Calcite)

Pink Magnesium Calcite is also known as Manganoan Calcite or Mangano Calcite. This is a stone of peace and well-being, and of universal love. It combines not only the heart healing properties of its various shades of pinks, but the grounding, cleansing and energizing power of Calcite. It is a delicious looking stone, and has a lovely gentle and nurturing feel to it, and reminds me of pink ice-cream.

Due to its ability to bring the flow of energy from the Crown Chakra down into the Heart Chakra, Pink Calcite can attract new opportunities to learn the concept of Universal Love. It is greatly beneficial for those enduring any type of emotional trauma, including abuse, the death of someone close or a break-up.

Those who suppress their emotions will benefit from Pink ManganoCalcite's ability to bring out deep-seated causes for acknowledgment, release and ultimately, healing.

This delicious pink and white stone is a calming gem that eases and heals the heart Chakra. It fills the heart with universal love and self-love, which enhances the opportunities and likelihood of romantic love, as well as bringing a centering and grounding to the love experience.

Some refer to this as "Reiki Stone" but it is a stone for any form of energy healing or energy channeling work. It can assist in energy work (Ki-Force, Reiki, Pranic Healing etc) by allowing the healing vibrations to travel to the right location on the client.

It has a gentle but powerful energy, and is an excellent complement to energy healing modalities because of its excellent properties of energy magnification. Pink Calcite is also extremely helpful for long distance healers because of its ability to amplify energy.

It has the ability to clear the nadis (energy channels) between the Crown and Heart Chakras and enhancing the flow of energy, clearing the emotional centre of stagnant or negative energies. This further allows for room for new experiences of Divine Love.

In crystal healings Pink ManganoCalcite is said to be beneficial for general health and healing, bones, joints, kidney, uterus, and physical heart issues. Physically, Pink ManganoCalcite is beneficial for general health and healing, bones, joints, and physical hearts. It is a stone of universal love.

This unique pink stone can be used to boost self-confidence and self-esteem as well as enhance compassion toward others. It offers hope for the best. ManganoCalcite heals inner child hurts and past abuse by filling one with a sense of motherly love.

This nurturing crystal assists us take care of ourselves as it enables us to not only accept love and be willing to experience self-love, but also to act on this with loving behaviors. It is a high powered stress reliever that relieves anxiety, stress and tension. It has been used to remove fears of all kinds and reduces nightmares.

Pebbles of it held in the hand can bring moments of comfort easily and delightfully.

Keywords for Pink ManganoCalcite are Universal Love, Compassion, Healing, Spiritualized Emotions.

31. Rhodochrosite

This is the "Stone of Love and Balance".

Rhodochrosite is a gentle crystal and is usually elegant pale rose-pink, deep pink, red or orangish-pink that often has bands of white. When it is banded it can be polished to display charming patterns and unique designs. Sometimes called Raspberry Spar, Rhodochrosite is a beautiful and attractive gem, whether in gem or jewelry form or in tumbled or carved pieces.

It is a gentle, yet loving stone to heal the Heart Chakra, and is probably the most vibrant loving stone for giving and receiving love. It assists with issues of romantic love and eases loneliness, loss, heartache, fear and insecurity.

It has a stronger energy than Rose Quartz and can be used for working with supporting and comforting the issues within the subconscious. Rhodochrosite can ease emotional pain and regenerate the heart and one's true identity bringing healing and self love.

Those dealing with loss will find a deep love within this stone as it helps to heal emotional wounds and hearts in trauma. Because it is comforting and positive, Rhodochrosite helps to bring repressed emotions to the surface to be acknowledged, addressed, and released, allowing for much personal growth to take place.

Rhodochrosite aids in self-forgiveness and self-love.

It is also known to work with and heal inner-child issues, as well as abuse or incest.

The ability to help with issues of self- forgiveness, deservingness and trust make this a truly healing stone. Because of its energy to bring compassion, comfort and a sense of being deeply loved, it can support one's spiritual nature, nurturing true self-love and creating the desire to live again.

Rhodochrosite balances and enhances love on all levels. It allows fuller love to enter one's life and assists in calming excessive passions. It helps to balance the mental and emotional processes and is claimed to be a stone of freedom because of its abilities to balance inner conflicts which serves to bring a deep sense of happiness and relief from ongoing stress.

Rhodochrosite is said to enhance creativity and to bring peace and tranquility during meditation. It is thought to be good crystal for relationships, especially for those who feel unloved, and is believed to be valuable in attracting a soul mate.

Many healers work with Rhodochrosite to bring much needed Love into the world.

It is often used for repairing the subtle bodies and for reclaiming lost gifts as working with Rhodochrosite can bring about the healing of past events that have caused the breakdown of one's self-confidence.

It aligns one with one's purpose again. This self-knowledge can assist one to see where personal gifts have been given up due to being challenged by life events or where they have been living in "survival mode". Once these past issues are healed, it can become easier to remember one's gifts again and their true purpose for this incarnation.

It also assists with accessing nurturing earth energy after undergoing transformation experiences, supporting integration on all levels, particularly in the heart centre.

Physically, Rhodochrosite heals the heart, adjusts imbalances in the circulatory and nervous systems, relieves migraines, and clears up infections.

Keep Rhodochrosite in the bedroom to help with sexual issues.

Rhodochrosite is good for exhaustion arising from frustration.

It can help to increase energy and to bring balance and stability to the heart Chakra as well as for the physical body.

Keywords: Love and Balance, Heart healer.

32. Rose Quartz

The "Love Stone".

This amazing stone has a translucent and peaceful feeling to it. It is a quartz of pinkish hues, the colours ranging from pale pink to deep rose and often appears to be a mix of opaque and transparency. It often has a chunky feel to it, unless it has been polished into form as a heart, pebble or other decorative design.

It always feels comfortable to the touch and comforting to hold, emitting a gentle love energy that seems to take the edge off the harshness of life. It often looks milky in appearance and brings a soothing and cooling energy.

Rose Quartz is known the world over as a stone of unconditional love. It opens the heart Chakra to all forms of love: self-love, family love, platonic love, and romantic love. Bringing gentleness and kindness into any space, it elevates the energy of ordinary quartz and combines the rose color of the heart to give the energy for enhancing love in virtually any situation. And relationship. It brings gentleness, forgiveness, and tolerance. Rose quartz is associated with the heart Chakra.

Rose quartz feels like a nurturing friend and enhances self esteem, self acceptance and self gentleness. It carries a happy and loving energy.

It is the ideal stone to reduce stress and trauma. Self image and self confidence are increased, and compassion and patience for the self and for others are enhanced.

The unconditional energy of Rose Quartz help us to learn to love our self more fully which ultimately helps us to reach out in love to others. The heart is harmonized and intimacy is encouraged and sustained as it gently soothes and warms the heart centre.

Through its gentleness and acceptance, self discipline is fostered and the barriers to self responsibility and the holding on to old fears are gently melted. Peacefulness and emotional balance are recharged as emotional states are cleansed and realigned. The energy bodies are realigned especially the mental, emotional and astral bodies. Uncomfortable memories are more easily discarded or disassembled.

A sense of beauty and balance are invited to share its space and because it is so effective at clearing inharmonious energies needs to be cleared often. Soothing to sleep with, a simple but thorough rinse with water in the morning can refresh and clear its energies to support you again through the night.

It possesses all the qualities of quartz crystal, however it is transduced into a very gentle yet steady stream of manageable energy that supports all levels of the being, not just the heart.

It is known to ease the process of dying, making a more gentle transition.

Keyword is "Stone of Love".

33. Rubellite (Pink or Red Tourmaline)

Rubellite is also known as Red Tourmaline even though it can range from pink to deep red and is a stone of the perfected heart. The name Rubellite comes from the Latin rubellus meaning "reddish," and refers to the similarity of its color to that of the Ruby, though Rubellite is not connected with Ruby but is part of the Tourmaline family.

Most Rubellites are more pink than red. They vary in hue from pale to shocking pink to a bold ruby-red, sometimes with a violet tint. True Rubellite shines just as intensely in artificial light as it does in daylight.

Tourmaline itself is a powerful, electromagnetic striated gem. The section on Tourmaline gives you further information on the properties of this powerful stone. Tourmaline assists in improving self-esteem and to restore the correct functioning of mind and body again.

Pink or red Rubellite has a high Lithium content which helps to bring emotional balance, lovingness and devotion in a down-to-earth way.

Rubellite draws upon Universal Love for healing the heart, and suggests that "heartbreak" can be "heart-opening," and grief can possibly be as valuable as joy. For those who are emotionally numb, Rubellite provides the way back into feeling once again, and allows for those who have become passive to rediscover their zest for living. It is strongly associated with the Heart and Root Chakra.

It can link not only to the heart of the Earth, but opens to love that goes beyond human relationships and reaches out to the Universe.

Rubellite stimulates not only the Heart Chakra, but also the Root Chakra, bringing an increased flow of *prana*, or life-force energies which nurture and help heal the emotional body. It also has a grounding influence that increases a zest for living as well as increasing the desire and ability for lively interaction with others.

In the home or office, Rubellite Tourmaline can help to neutralize the harmful electromagnetic effects of microwaves, computers and other electronics. It can also deter people from picking fights or disputing one's expertise as it can help to bestow the energy of dignity, diplomacy and quiet authority when others are being unreasonable or pulling rank.

Rubellite may also be used for harmonizing the feminine energies within both sexes, and lends strength to women in emotional challenges.

Pink Tourmaline is such a pretty stone when in polished gem form, and gives a gentle yet very powerful energy that supports healing in all areas to do with the heart.

It brings its own innate protection to the heart, so that it can address any past injuries and move past them to be able to embrace true love again. The emotional heart is soothed helping to overcome hidden fears concerning the issues of abundance, survival, stability and safety, and supports those who feel isolated or have difficulty in feeling at home in the world.

Pink tourmaline is good for attracting love in both the material and spiritual world. It helps the wearer to see that it is safe to love, and confirms that it is necessary to love oneself first before one can hope to be loved by others.

Pink tourmaline helps to ground, strengthen and rejuvenate the wearer or user and offsets stress.

When the pink variety is combined with green tourmaline in the Watermelon Tourmaline, it can allow a sense of lightness and humour in serious situations.

Red Tourmaline strengthens, grounds, rejuvenates and warms.

It aids to unite the heart and body again and as a result it enhances love, passion and courage, increasing energy, stamina and steadiness.

It also balances the body's electrochemistry. Part of its gift is to help detach from personal pain. It has been known to assist in releasing reproductive blocks and to stimulate fertility.

Some use this stone to strengthen and detoxify the blood and immune system. It is also said to ease radiation effects.

It has a Yang energy.

Keywords: Heart Healer, Will Power.

34. Ruby

Natural Ruby is one of the four "precious" gemstones (Diamond, Ruby, Emerald and Sapphire) known for their rarity, monetary value, and has a hardness second only to Diamond. Many consider this to be the most magnificent of all gems, the queen of stones and the stone of kings. It was considered by the Ancients to be of value exceeded even by that of the Diamond and that its virtue surpassed all other precious stones. Interestingly it is a main centrepiece on the Imperial State Crown used for British Coronation ceremonies.

It is a fiery and captivating blood-red stone of nobility and inspires passion and an enthusiasm for life. The bright red is caused by the presence of the element chromium, and its name comes from *ruber* which is Latin for red. When it is its polished form, it can be like living fire. Unpolished it is just as effective for healing and energy work.

All natural Rubies have imperfections within them, including color impurities and inclusions of Rutile needles known as "silk." These inclusions help distinguish natural Ruby from synthetics and when structurally oriented so the light shines off the "silk" in certain ways, the inclusions actually increase the rarity and value of the stone. If cut as a cabochon, these special stones may display a chatoyancy, or rare "cat's eye" effect, or in the case of a Star Ruby may display a six-rayed star effect called asterism, that causes the light rays to appear to glide magically across the stone as it is moved.

This precious gem is energetically valuable even when in rough form. Polished it has a brilliant energy to it and becomes very high powered. Great fire can spark from its depths. It was once considered more precious than diamond though this seems to have changed in public opinion over the last couple of hundred years.

Ruby brings integrity, devotion and happiness. It also enhances generosity and brings prosperity. It was once a favourite for love gifts and for engagements when affordable.

Ruby brings and increases romantic love. Primarily Ruby symbolizes beauty, passion, power, deep love, strength and devotion. It supports love and passion in relationships as well as bringing wealth, joy, love, sexual energy and power.

It is a stone of high energy and power that can promote healing on all levels.

Ruby is associated with the root Chakra. Ruby can improve motivation and the setting of realistic goals, whilst encouraging joy, spontaneity, laughter and courage. It is said to balance the heart and inspire confidence in day to day affairs.

Ruby is also thought to promote positive dream states for some, bringing good dreams, and restful nights. It is considered to aid in maintaining wealth and passion and was once called "the Merchant's Stone". Ruby encourages removal of negative energies from your path and helps with overcoming exhaustion and lethargy, bringing positive energy and motivation. It is also claimed to be helpful in calming hyperactivity, in children and adults alike.

In physical healing it is thought that Ruby detoxifies the body, blood and lymphatic system. It treats circulatory disorders, fevers and fights off infectious diseases. Warms and energizes after periods of exhaustion and strengthens physical and emotional heart.

Though if you are a Sensitive going through upsets and are around a lot of anger, this stone will either give you the energy and strength to combat it, or make you angrier or more tired, so be aware and discerning when using it in this way. It has been my experience that if you are very sensitive and have adrenal exhaustion, it can initiate and support extra energy and action temporarily and to a degree but care must be taken not to overextend your energetic activity as there may be a false sense of one's true energy supplies.

Limit your use of this energetically motivating stone and allow recovery time between uses. As it can bring anger or negativity to the surface quickly, it should be used with the knowledge of how to gain from the experience or you are likely to be overcome by the passion it stirs up. Consider working with adrenal strengthening nutritional or herbal support to fully maximize the effects and potentials of this powerful gem.

Star Ruby has the same metaphysical properties as Ruby, but with increased healing and magical energies. It is most powerful at full moon. It may also be more suitable for the Sensitive as it brings a greater degree of protection. The Light of the Soul is reflected and grounded within the star of the Ruby, and amplifies one's internal resources and fortitude.

It is extremely potent for those inclined to self-harm or self-neglect, and is quite beneficial in overcoming sexual dysfunction or the trauma of sexual or power abuse and suppressed anger. As a stone of spiritual Light, it can be used by Light workers and healers to integrate high-frequency energy into the body, and assists one in recognizing the true abundance of life.

Keywords for Ruby are: Abundance, Spiritual Balance, Courage, Passion.

35. Rutilated Quartz

Rutilated Quartz can often look as though beautiful clear quartz crystal has been laced with golden threads or rods in a way that makes them look like frozen angel hair. These golden threads which have often been called "The Hairs of Venus" can range from rutiles of copper or appear silvery or blue-grey from titanium dioxide fibres. Rutilated Quartz emits a very high energy frequency and intensifies the powers of quartz. This affects the etheric and astral bodies and acts as a link between the Base Chakra and the Crown Chakra. The rutiles are powerful electrical conductors and amplify energy, thoughts and crystal programming. They assist in strengthening the energy bodies and support the regeneration of these as well as physical tissue throughout body.

This combination is a powerful healer. The Golden fibres are thought to increase radiation protection as well as to promote healthy rejuvenation. The rutiles heighten whatever energetic influence the regular quartz already possesses and helps direct that boosted energy to the problematic areas. Any codes are greatly amplifies. For energy regeneration and transference, this is a gem for all Chakras.

Rutilated Quartz is an uplifting stone, infusing joy into one's life and surrounding environment.

This type of quartz promotes precision alignment with Higher Sources of energy and inspiration to help us physically anchor the ability to access, synthesize, and communicate information from other dimensions and realms. It inspires connection with the highest spiritual levels. Rutile in the Quartz, acts as a kind of psychic antenna.

The golden or silver color of Rutilated Quartz works very well for manifestation programs. The holder can imagine themselves within the crystal to program it, vividly imagining the energies of the program moving along the individual Rutiles.

For some this quartz can make one too spacey or scattered to wear as it induces Alpha states and can enhance communication with higher self and spirit guides as well as to increase clairvoyance. So it is suggested to be worn or used with something more grounding such as Smoky Quartz, Onyx or Tourmaline etc.

Rutile is also known to make up the extremely fine threads that cause the stars in ruby and sapphire, and can also form in topaz and tourmaline. Today, the vast majority of Rutilated Quartz is mined in Brazil, but it is also found in most of the major gem producing nations.

Rutilated Quartz also enhances self-reliance and helps with decision-making.

Keywords for Rutilated Quartz are: Spiritual Inspiration, Aura Protector and Energizer, Childhood Issues, Rejuvenator.

36. Smoky Quartz

Smokey Quartz / Smoky Quartz is a stone of protection and grounding.

The colours range from a transparent pale hint of brown to a translucent dark brown or to a very dark almost black brown and even when totally transparent it can appear to have a slightly smoky appearance to it. Until one sees a Smoky Quartz, this may sound very dull and uninspiring. But it is actually a very beautiful stone, particular if it has some shade lines or striations in it. When cut into gem shape, it takes on a lovely soft beauty.

In esoteric circles, it has been associated with protection from negative energies. This may be because negative energies like to hang out where there is a lot of fear, and Smoky Quartz assists with transforming or removing emotional blockages, particularly fear and restrictions. It is also believed to help support and protect against environmental pollution, radiation and electromagnetic smog. Smoky Quartz can help to reduce stress.

Smoky Quartz is well known as a grounding stone, which means that it helps to keep one practical, and to assist in "anchoring" one's energy work into the physical realm. It combines all of the properties of normal quartz with the color of the earth to allow this action. It's considered to be one of the Abundance crystals, assisting in bringing your dreams and plans into manifestation, particularly when focusing on one's goals with clear intent. As it assists in clearing emotional blocks, this helps to make way for positive energies to support your intentions.

It is said that due to its Sodium content, which contributes to its dark colour, Smoky Quartz can assist to regulate the fluid levels within the body. When one considers that there is a high water content in the body, and that the body requires a variety of mineral salts to function correctly, then this makes sense. It would also seem that this crystal can vibrate to help balance these salts in the body.

According to certain sources, in Chinese Medicine, there are energy channels throughout the body known as meridians. Smoky Quartz assists in balancing the meridians in the hands and feet, which are related to many of the organs and systems of the body. This then can contribute to physical balance of the body energies.

Because of its association with Abundance, Smoky Quartz can help one's focus, and assist with mental clutter. It is a stone of serenity and helpful for encouraging courage and inner fortitude.

If you are on a spiritual journey, then know that this stone can help to keep you grounded, as one may possibly become ungrounded after meditation or when doing a lot of intense mental, psychic or energy work.

Smoky Quartz is often used in healing energy work alongside other crystals to help to ground the actions and capabilities of other healing stones. It also provides a safer space to work in. It is related to the base Chakra, the kidneys and adrenals, and the stomach.

For Energy Workers, it helps to provide an anchoring type of energy, and to help center ones energy. This supports the energies of both the client and the worker, and enhance the flow of Life Force Energy for the energy treatment.

And of course, for the best healing results and before you work on anyone else, you always work on your own heart and life first. This stone can assist you to clear your own energy blockages, and to be more real and consequently more powerful in your life and in your authenticity.

Some Smoky Quartz was originally ordinary clear or white-ish quartz crystal that has been irradiated to make it turn brown, and is usually a dense almost opaque black brown, rather than a clear or semi transparent brown.

Still as beautiful and sometimes possibly even more striking than the genuine or natural Smoky, it may be prized in jewelry, but may not be quite as powerful for energy work, though it is still effective. There is nothing wrong with obtaining this kind of quartz – just know what you are buying and don't allow yourself to be charged the same price for this inferior product.

Like clear or milky quartz, smoky quartz is an energy conductor and generator. Smoky quartz disperses negative patterns and vibrations, and transmits a high quantity of light.

- It purifies the primal instincts (1st Chakra)
- Helps one get in touch with nature
- Excellent for meditation and healing on the mental and etheric levels
- Smoky helps to reach the goals sent during psychic dreams, during which it increases awareness and helps to guide spirits in channeling dreams
- Transforms escapist attitudes and allows one to let go of what is not needed to allow growth
- Negative emotional energy
- Mood swings
- Aggressive actions,
- Ill temper
- Generally nasty thoughts
- Grounds all kinds of negative energy
- Helpful for burnout
- Fear of failure
- Reluctance to take risks
- Wanting revenge

- Tendencies to over-eat, smoke or drink due to stress
- Helps acceptance of responsibility for self
- Broadens capacity for effective communication by dissolving self-limiting perceptions

It can be used to gently dissolve negative energies and emotional blockages. It can be used to initiate a powerful force field which will absorb many forms of negativity, both from within one's self and from other forces. It promotes personal pride and joy in living.

Smoky quartz has been used to regulate creativity in business, and to encourage astute-ness in purchasing. It works to diffuse communication deficiencies and to dissolve mental and emotional blockages that limit perception and learning.

Keywords for Smoky Quartz are: Grounding, Balance, Protection, Business. Some sources cite its abilities with Kundalini Energy.

37. Snowflake Obsidian

Obsidian is usually a black and almost brittle stone, and has a highly polished surface. It absorbs and disperses negativity and can also reduce stress. It can also come in other colours such as green and blue where it is almost transparent and may appear somewhat like glass. Other colours are brown and there are the layered varieties of rainbow, silver and gold obsidian. These look stunning when polished into shapes that show off the layering to advantage.

Obsidian is a volcanic glass and is an excellent grounding stone. It shields against negativity and can disperse unloving thoughts. It also aids detachment and can absorb anger and fear, converting it to white light. It is a great stone for providing gentle protection from evil intent. Black Obsidian can also provide energy to other crystals, particularly those that are damaged.

Its energy can initiate deep change and can do this quickly, yet it also seems to provide the support that is required to integrate the changes that it initiates. It is a wonderful healer as it addresses the deep and hidden and the impact of its energy cannot be denied. Allows one to recognise the unnecessary patterns that remain in one's life and to change the thought that makes those patterns. I have lived in a place that was built on a huge slab of obsidian, and whilst there it quickly brought issues up to the surface that I had buried but that had to be faced in order to be resolved. But its energy also gave me the nurturing and support to get through them whilst grounding me. I also felt protected whilst undergoing the changes and associated transformations.

Obsidian is a stone of purity for the mind, body and spirit, providing balance whilst assisting in recognition of stressful mental patterns. It helps to centre oneself, and assists in accepting or viewing isolation and loneliness differently, so that they become empowering.

The Snowflake variety has a gentler energy and has deposits within it that appear to be circular and the interesting and often pretty patterns of the "snowflakes" against the black of the obsidian can give the impression of melting snowflakes within the stone. It feels smooth and soothing to the touch, and has a nurturing as well as strengthening sense. This is one of my favourite crystals, with its friendly and warm feeling, one which seems to give strength, as well as gentleness. Snowflake Obsidian promotes self-esteem and confidence. It promotes Clairaudience and the owning of one's lower aspects for growth.

Snowflake Obsidian encourages inner reflection making us aware of negative patterns of thought and unhealthy patterns of behaviour and giving us the chance to change them.

It is also believed to help shield the wearer from negativity and grief. It can help to focus ones inner vision, and provide blunt answers on the correct course of action to take. It aids in speeding up serious self development processes.

In healing Snowflake Obsidian is believed to improve the circulation and to benefit the skin and veins. Snowflake Obsidian has a restful and serene energy helping to bring peace and balance to the mind and body.

Keywords are Transformation, Protection, Healthy Balance.

38. Star Sapphire

Blue Sapphire ranges in hue from pale to deep azure or dark royal blue, to indigo, with the most highly desired color being the velvety cornflower blue, also called Kashmir or bleu de roi. The name Sapphire is derived from the Latin sapphirus, Greek sappheiros, and Sanskrit sanipryam, meaning "blue stone." Recent research indicates that what we know today as Lapis Lazuli was also referred to as Sapphire in the ancient world.

The magnificent Sapphire, in all its celestial hues, is known as a stone of wisdom and royalty, and also of prophecy and Divine favour. It has been associated since ancient times with sacred things and was considered the gem of gems, a jewel connected with nearly every religion.

To many of the ancient and medieval world, Sapphire of heavenly blue signified the height of celestial hope and faith, and was believed to bring protection, good fortune and spiritual insight. It was not only a symbol of power and strength, but also of kindness and wise judgment.

Sapphire supports devotion to one's divine purpose and can help to synchronize the energy systems with one's higher purpose. It is said to intensify the qualities of loyalty and responsibility to one's true work on the planet.

In Hebrew lore, King Solomon and Abraham both wore talismans of Sapphire, and the Law given to Moses on the Mount was said by some to be engraved on tablets of Sapphire, not Emerald.

As a talisman, Sapphire was thought to preserve chastity, assist in discovering fraud and treachery, protect its wearer from poison, plague, fever and skin diseases, and had great power in resisting black magic and ill-wishing.

It is claimed to have healed ailments of the eyes, as well as to increase concentration.

Today Sapphire is still a Stone of Wisdom, a royal stone of learning, mental acuity and psychic activation, a seeker after spiritual truth. Its pure Blue Ray brings order and healing to the mind, lending strength and focus, and an ability to see beneath surface appearances to underlying truths and to utilize that knowledge.

Blue Sapphire embraces order, structure, and self-discipline, and is ideal for accomplishing goals and manifesting ideas into form. Sapphire's power to transmute negative thoughts and energy also makes it highly effective for earth and Chakra healing.

Sapphire stimulates the Throat and Third Eye Chakras. It allows one to access deeper levels of consciousness in order to gain a fuller understanding of the self.

Because Sapphire stimulates the third eye it opens us to our spiritual nature by relaxing tension and anxiety and the gem essence imparts the gifts of wisdom, tranquility, loyalty and prophecy. It also works as a relaxing agent during times of extreme physical exertion.

Healers of the spirit and body are often drawn to this stone.

Star Sapphire has all the magnified qualities of the Blue Sapphire, but differs in that it has an aqueous inclusion in its makeup that creates a refracted six-pointed star on the stone's surface. This star is a major focus point in the gem. The Star is formed through the intergrowth of fibrous inclusions of Rutile "silk," that reflects light in stones cut as cabochon. This displays the six-rayed or sometimes twelve-rayed star that appears to glide across the face of the gem as it is moved. This effect is called asterism and increases the rarity and value of the stone.

The star itself represents the manifestation of Divine knowledge and Light into denser reality, and reminds us that the outer manifestations we treasure are a reflection of the Light of our own essence. The three lines that cross in the six-rayed star represent faith, hope and destiny, sometimes associated with three angels who offer protection to those who wear Star Sapphire. The moving star brings ongoing safety to travelers and guides their way home.

It is associated with the planet Saturn, and for this reason is used in Vedic astrology to offset the impact of this planet at each Saturn Return, which is approximately every 27-28 years of one's life.

Star Sapphire assists in promoting trust in the universe and can help us focus our awareness on what is necessary for the soul's progression in life. It can also support the formation of energetic connections that support the realization of our life goals.

Keywords are: Balances the Chakras, Soul Progression.

39. Sunstone

Sunstone is a joyful stone. It sparkles like a thousand warm and glowing diamond glints in a burned toffee or sand-coloured smooth stone. It has a unique gold-orange metallic sheen and the tiny Hematite crystals it contains add sparkle and fire and can produce an iridescent effect as the stone is viewed from various angles. It appears to pick up any light around and to reflect it back, bringing in the power of the sun.

Sunstone is a stone of personal power and reflects many positive attributes, bringing with it abundance and good luck as well as the power to "shine".

With its powerful connection to the light and power of the sun, Sunstone brings light to situations. Its bright and joyful energy increases vitality and helps to lighten dark moods. It also helps with feelings of abandonment or persecution as it assists in instilling confidence and optimism together with positive action.

Sunstone increases vitality, lifts the spirits and aids in psychic work. It offsets stress and depression as it is associated with chi or life force and is useful for removing energy drains or hooks into your energy by others.

Sunstone can lift depressive moods and bring in more joy and beauty of life. This is beneficial for S.A.D. (Seasonal Affective Disorder) when there is little sun around. Because this stone encourages optimism, it enhances the ability to value and nurture the self.

It has also been claimed to provide a source of strength when experiencing loss or over dependency.

The mind and energy fields benefit from the connection to the Sunstone energy as it helps with providing rest from stressful thoughts and emotions.

It encourages optimism and enthusiasm and helps overcome procrastination, helping you take action to live your life as you'd like to now.

Sunstone helps you develop your own originality, encourages independence and alleviates fearfulness. It is said to bring good fortune and abundance.

As Sunstone is associated with the Solar Plexus Chakra, it can assist in unblocking this Chakra connected with weight problems around the middle, as well as digestive issues, irritable bowel syndrome and even stomach ulcers. Some claim that it speeds metabolism. It warms the heart and rejuvenates the spirit.

Sunstone has the capacity to energize all Chakras.

Sunstone is highly effective in cleansing the aura and Chakras, and for removing hooks from possessive loved ones, lovers, or anyone draining of your energies.

Sunstone surrounds these hooks with love and positive energy, and returns them to their source. It is especially beneficial when ties need to be cut, or if you have difficulty saying "No". It helps remove co-dependency, overcome procrastination, and encourages self-empowerment and independence.

Those who hold back because of fears and self-doubt may find Sunstone melts away the sense of unworthiness, feelings of being discriminated against, disadvantaged or abandoned.

It emanates a rich and positive spectrum of energies that re-balances one's emotional patterns, and encourages optimism and enthusiasm. It can help transform anger into energy and judgment into joy.

When worn as a pendant, Sunstone can bring the heart's wisdom into alignment with the mind's inspirations.

Sunstone is an abundance stone.

It encourages independence and originality, is inspirational in revealing talents, and attracts fame and unexpected prosperity. It is an excellent "good luck" crystal for competitions. If you seek recognition, wear Sunstone as it's said to draw fame to you.

Keywords for Sunstone are Inner Strength, Joy, Vitality, Empowerment.

40. Tigers Eye

This silky-smooth stone has amazing lustres and lights held within. It brings a feeling of warmth with its deep golden and brown colours, and is entrancing with its traces of silky threads that run throughout it.

It is a yellow-brown, semiprecious chatoyant gemstone consisting of quartz with parallel veins of silicified altered crocidolite. "Chatoyancy" exhibits a changeable silky lustre as light is reflected within the thin parallel fibrous bands. This effect is due to the fibrous structure of the material.

Tigers Eye is a stone of good luck, wealth and courage. It is said to bring passion and physical strength to the carrier. Tiger Eye attracts abundance.

Tiger Eye is one of the best gemstones to manifest one's thoughts into reality as it enhances the connection with personal power and will as well as providing emotional balance. It can help one see how to create heaven on earth. Tiger Eye is an excellent stone to stay balanced, focused, and centred, whilst also being grounding. It helps develop intuition and psychic ability. It is a good stone to uplift the spirit in times of depression.

Tiger or Tiger's Eye is great for those who are afraid of success. It enhances self empowerment and strengthens the energetic boundary between our true natures and our emotional experiences. It also helps us maintain a strong sense of self identity when dealing with powerful emotions such as anger, fear, and jealousy

Tiger Eye seems to bring together the vibrations of sand and sunlight. This combination of the energies of sun and earth bring stability and dynamic beauty. For those who get too involved with 'details', it helps when seeking clarity. It can also be used to enhance psychic abilities as well as to better attune the third eye.

Because of its Earth and Sun energy, Golden Brown Tiger Eye draws spiritual energy down to the Earth, while still keeping you centered here on the ground. Tiger Eye helps to raise vibrations, while also connecting these higher energies to the lower Chakras. It brings brightness and optimism to a situation, keeping you balanced and connected when working with higher goals.

Known as a stone of protection, especially for travelers, Tiger Eye brings good luck and prosperity to the user. Ancients used Tiger Eye as a talisman against bad luck and curses.

Brown/Golden Tiger Eye is a powerful Solar Plexus Chakra stone, helpful in manifesting ideas into reality and giving courage in times of change. Use Golden Brown Tiger Eye with the Solar Plexus Chakra to increase your personal power. With intention, surround a lit green candle with Tiger Eye to attract prosperity.

Tiger's Eye is a stone of protection and was traditionally carried as a talisman against ill wishes and curses. It is both a grounding and uplifting crystal and can encourage feelings of self-worth and confidence in our own abilities. It can promote a positive attitude, assist us in accomplishing our goals and help us to recognise our own talents and abilities.

Tiger's Eye is also said to enhance our personal empowerment as well as to release blocked creativity, it also brings good luck, prosperity, wealth and success together with a joyful outlook and sunny disposition. Tiger's Eye supports the Solar Plexus Chakra.

As a good luck stone, it can also be used for protection.

Blue Tiger Eye calms and aids in releasing stress. It can also assist the quick-tempered, overanxious and phobic.

It has also been used to slow the metabolism.

Red Tigers Eye has the similar properties to Gold Tiger's Eye and is very good at motivation to those feeling tired or exhausted.

Red Tigers Eye is also very effective at boosting a flagging libido and when placed under the pillow has been claimed to summon motivation for a more passionate sex life

Earthy, grounding. optimism, insight, personal power.

Overall keywords are Personal Power and Higher Purpose.

41. Topaz

Topaz generally comes in blues, greens and radiant yellow-gold, though it can also be clear or amberish. Blue Topaz may be true blue or it may be irradiated to be the brilliant blue we often see adorning rings.

Topaz is an amazing stone, and is often referred to as the stone of "true love and success in all endeavours". It is said that Topaz acts as a conductor of thought or desire, sending a message to the ethers. This mineral is the "crystal of potency", instrumental in expanding the energy of visualization and projection for healing or attracting. It seems to act through the laws of attraction and manifestation.

Used in healing or in meditation it helps clear energy blockages in the Solar Plexus. It also helps to tap into appropriate sources of universal energy. It can strengthen the ability to act decisively from a clear sense of personal identity. Topaz is perfect for those avoiding making a decision which would commit one to a course of action. It assists when there is a loss of willpower through lack of ability to make a decision.

Topaz sends out positive energy to all who need it, and is excellent for those in crisis or in need of motivation. It recharges and increases the user's energy level. It benefits those who are problem solvers, such as those involved with the arts or science. It is an excellent stone for relaxation and for comfort and it calms the nervous system and lessens tension. Topaz also benefits the blood.

Topaz sheds light on the path to your goals. Those in tune with Topaz's positive energy will feel limitless and philanthropic. They will experience an increase in their personal abilities. It is also a stone of positive attraction.

Topaz can be used to manifest health and to help correct disorders within the body. It promotes understanding, compassion, kindness and empathy. Any variety of Topaz can open and heal the hearts of those who have closed them while also protecting the open-hearted from too much pain. This assists in attracting and holding love in relationships. It is instrumental in visualizations for healing and attracting in meditation and projection. Topaz helps one to creatively change their personal world, enhance awareness, promote expansiveness and increase manifestation.

In crystal healing Topaz is best known for its manifesting properties, it is a crystal of joy, generosity, abundance and good health. It is known as a stone of love and good fortune, and is said to release tension and encourage relaxation.

It promotes openness and honesty, self-realisation and self-control, stabilises the emotions, making you receptive to love from all sources.

Topaz is a lovely soothing, regenerating and stimulating crystal. It balances the meridians of the body, directing energy to where it is needed most. It assists with finding solutions to problems and in expressing ideas.

Topaz assists in physical healing by aiding digestion and helps combat eating disorders, such as anorexia.

Blue Topaz: It stimulates and activates the throat Chakra, cleansing and supporting the spoken word and self expression. Blue Topaz brings truth and wisdom; it aids in clear communication and helps one to recognise where they have strayed from their own truth. It can assist to promote truth and forgiveness.

It is a very soothing and calming stone and can distance one from stress and problems by raising the vibratory rate and allowing one to rise above them.

It is useful for problem solving or sorting out muddled feeling and ideas.

It can inspire and uplift and promote truth, honesty, openness and forgiveness. It can help one to discover their own inner riches and help to find and attain your goals.

In summary, Topaz prime energies are support success, true love, individuality, creativity and joy.

Yellow-Golden Topaz keywords: Spiritual Rebirth, "Stone of True Love and Success in All Endeavours".

42. Tourmaline

This stone generally appears as an opaque shiny, dense and lengthwise striated Black crystal. It is most representative in thick shards or wands and can be quite thick in girth. You will also find it as a pebble, as well as fashioned into shapes, though you might also be lucky to find it as big chunks of longish shards embedded in another crystal matrix such as quartz. Black tourmaline is generally opaque, but the coloured varieties of tourmaline can be opaque or clear and polished in gem quality pieces.

All tourmaline assists in transforming dense energies into a lighter vibration. It grounds, clears and balances and assists in pointing to solutions.

It is a powerful, electromagnetic striated gem. It strengthens body and spirit (and meridians), transmutes lower frequency thought or energy to a higher frequency of light and brings light/spirit into the physical. Tourmaline radiates light and protection for the wearer. It does not absorb negative energy and is helps clear to a higher frequency.

It is especially good for the nervous system, the blood and for clearing lymph toxins. It is suggested to carry this stone when you feel surrounded by negativity.

This is a valuable stone for crises and for periods of extreme stress. It also helps to defend against debilitating diseases. It is also strongly suggested for persons with weakened immune systems. Tourmaline transforms dense energy into a lighter vibration, and forms a protective shield around the body. As well as promoting self confidence it also assists to banish feelings of being a victim.

It attracts inspiration, tolerance and prosperity.

One of Tourmaline's most distinguishing properties is its ability to become electrically charged simply by heating or rubbing it.

When charged, one end becomes positive and the other negative, allowing it to attract particles of dust or bits of paper. This property of pyroelectricity (from heat) or piezoelectricity (from pressure or rubbing) was well-known to the Dutch traders of the 1700s.

Although Tourmaline may be found on every continent, fine crystal specimens and gems are still considered rare and can be quite expensive.

Its vast popularity as a gemstone began in 1876, when mineralogist and jeweller George Kunz sold a Green Tourmaline from Maine to the famous Tiffany and Co. in New York, and its desirability spread.

More recently it has become a favourite of metaphysical collectors and practitioners for its versatile energy properties.

Tourmaline strengthens the sense of smell, and in that respect, can also enhance the perception of pheromones which produces an aphrodisiac effect. Tourmaline promotes self understanding and right-left brain hemisphere balance.

Black tourmaline is protective against cell phones, electromagnetic smog, radiation, psychic attack, spells and ill-wishing etc.

It can allow clear rational thought and objective neutrality.

Tourmalated / Tourmalinated Quartz /Quartz containing Tourmaline shards:

Combines the qualities of quartz and tourmaline. This combination assists in releasing patterns destructive to one's life. Gives one the strength to solve unhealthy relationships and situations.

Some keywords for Tourmaline:

> Tourmaline, Black (Schorl) - Protection
>
> Tourmaline, Blue (Indicolite) - Expression
>
> Tourmaline, Blue-Green - Loving Expression
>
> Tourmaline, Cat's Eye - Visions
>
> Tourmaline, Chrome - Heart Opening
>
> Tourmaline, Green - Paternal Issues
>
> Tourmaline, Quartz - Spiritual Unfoldment
>
> Tourmaline, Red (Rubellite) - Will Power
>
> Tourmaline, Watermelon - Heart Alignment

Keywords for Tourmaline include: Transformation, Grounding, Clearing, Balancing.

43. Turquoise

Turquoise is often easy to recognize because of its obvious connection to the color with the same name. It can range from a light blue-green shade to a deep blue-green, and is an opaque stone, yet soothing to the touch and healing to the eye, as if carved from an azure heaven that has slipped to earth. Its unique shades of green-blues and blue-greens, tends to all things of this tranquil hue. Sometimes it contains delicate veining or mottled webbing in cream or brown and this is inherent to the stone and serves to enhance its character.

The name Turquoise is derived from the French, 'pierre turquoise', meaning "Turkish stone". In times past there were trade routes that brought Turquoise to Europe from the mines in central Asia passing through Turkey, where Venetian merchants often purchased the stone in Turkish bazaars. Do not be taken in by a dyed version of Howlite, which does not have the same depth of real turquoise, even though it is often heavily dyed with the colour.

For thousands of years, Turquoise has been prized as a symbol of wisdom, nobility and the power of immortality. Among the Ancient Egyptians, Persians and Chinese, Aztecs and Incas of South America, and Native North Americans, Turquoise was sacred in its adornment and for power, luck, and protection. Turquoise beads have dated back to 5000 B.C. and the Egyptians were prolific in their use of this beautiful stone. The death mask of Tutankhamun was studded with Turquoise, as were the mosaic masks dedicated to the gods, including the fabulous inlaid skulls, shields and power statues of Moctezuma, the last ruler of the Aztecs.

Native Americans have mined and fashioned Turquoise for nearly a thousand years, using it to guard their burial sites. Indian priests wore it in ceremonies when calling upon the great spirit of the sky.

Many honoured Turquoise as the universal stone, believing their minds would become one with the universe when wearing it. Because of its ability to change colours, it was used in prophesy or divining.

Turquoise is an eye-catching stone and often brings an immediate visual lift. It is a good general healer for all illnesses and excellent conductor due to its high copper content.

This gentle, cool, soothing stone is a speech enhancer, and is perfect for enhancing all forms of friendship, communication and healing. It supports the Throat Chakra for clearer open communication and creativity, and gifts the wearer serenity, spiritual bonding and upliftment. It also opens the Heart Chakra for giving/receiving.

Turquoise symbolizes our source (spirit/sky) and spiritual love for healing. When worn on or decorating the brow it can indicate the desire for a Psychic connection to Great Spirit.

It strengthens and aligns all meridians, Chakras, subtle bodies and energy fields. Like amethyst, it protects and detoxifies from alcohol, poison, pollution, x-rays and sun radiation. It is an ancient absorber of "negativity"; and some say it provides protection from "evil eye."

Turquoise attunes the energy field to the ancient wisdom and sacredness inherent in all of life; cleanses and deepens our connection to the Soul of the earth; helps us live a life of simplicity. It is excellent for anxiety aggravated by darkness and for those who are seeking a way out of a problem but feel that there is as yet no solution.

It enhances and supports communication regarding emotional issues, creativity and intuition. It is also said to provide protection during astral travel, though these current times of huge change do not easily lend themselves to this once familiar form of self work. It is however, still effectively used for spiritual attunement, healing and cleansing the Chakras and physical body.

Turquoise has long been recognised as a protective stone and has been used throughout the ages for protective amulets. Today it is also believed to protect against outside influences and pollutants in the atmosphere. As a stone of purification, Turquoise dispels negative energy and clears electromagnetic smog from the environment.

It promotes self-realization and aids in creative problem-solving, thus calming the nerves when speaking in public. It also helps stabilize mood swings, and dissolves a martyred attitude of self-sabotage. It is also empowering if you feel bullied or suffer from prejudice. Because it soothes the mind, Turquoise is good for jet lag and fears of flying.

Turquoise can assist with creative problem solving and can calm the nerves when speaking in public. It is also believed to stabilise mood swings, dissolve self-sabotage and allow self-expression. Turquoise is good crystal to wear when you have decisions to make as it can encourage self-questioning.

This stone may be particularly beneficial for individuals who are seeking to heal other people, as simultaneous healing can occur. It also helps to clear the tendency to sympathetically take on others difficulties or characteristics.

Attunement to the stone may produce an increased confidence and trust in the healing process itself as a self-healing attribute can be activated bringing greater strength and energy.

When placed on the Throat Chakra, it can assist with releasing old vows or inhibitions, and allows the soul to express itself once more. Turquoise is a stone for finding wholeness and truth, and communicating and manifesting those qualities. Turquoise empowers those who are shy about sharing their understanding and aids in the knowledge that in speaking from the wholeness of our being, we each have something important to contribute to the collective.

Fades in sunlight, sweat, oil, dishwater. Avoid bleach/chlorine.

Keywords include: Master Healer, Deep understanding, Communication.

44. Verdelite (Green Tourmaline)

Green Tourmaline is also referred to as Verdelite, particularly in jewellery. Tourmaline itself is usually prismatic, vertically striated and often found in long and slender form, or thick and columnar. Natural formations are uniquely triangular in cross-section, and polish up beautifully, though they already have a lovely sheen.

One of Tourmaline's most distinguishing properties is its ability to become electrically charged simply by heating or rubbing it. This activates what is called pyroelectricity* and was once used for pulling ash-dust from pipes by Dutch traders in the 1700's. Put simply, it is capable of creating a positive and negative charge at opposite ends of its termination points.

High frequencies can be passed through Tourmaline without shattering it as other crystals might and is used in industry for conducting television and radio frequencies.

Combining this with the luscious power of green really harnesses and enhances the heart safely and gently. It brings a sense of gratitude, hope and renewal, and is never out of place in your crystal collection.

The power of green is harnessed in this stone and the many connections to green are worked with on a powerful level. Simply thinking of the colour Green can bring up those things that we associate with spring, new growth, hope, balance, nature-nurture, growth and fertility, creativity, progress, renewal, youth and health.

A deep green also works well for good finances, material comforts, prosperity, overcoming fear and increased good fortune. In this stone there is much effectiveness with progressing projects, productivity and success as well as strength and development.

Clear and good quality Tourmaline really enhances the power of green, and when faceted it can be a real powerhouse of these energies. It is a less expensive version than Emerald, but almost as powerful.

Verdelite is a wonderful crystal for working with the heart and the emotions. Because it is aligned through the green colour ray to the heart, a central point in the energy systems of man, and a major controlling point in the physical body, it will help with all emotional issues, including a sense of lack, loss or vulnerability.

Green Tourmaline helps protect the heart whilst it nurtures it.

When wearing a ring of this crystal, be aware that worn on the left hand will bring in the lovely energies toward you and your heart, but wearing it on the right hand will send out these energies to others. There is no right or wrong, just awareness of the action of this gem for your desired results.

The heart Chakra is enhanced and supported with this crystal, addressing fears and balancing us toward a better attitude towards life. The heart is better balanced, and has a greater perception if you like, as to what is best to embrace and what is wise to resist for one's happiness.

Energy Workers are aware that the heart plays a major role in the internal emotional and psychological balancing mechanisms that lead to healing many other ailments of discomforts and dis-ease in the body, so this crystal is really good for gentle yet powerful work.

Working with the Earth and Water elements, Green Tourmaline will enhance all associated meridians such as Kidneys, Bladder, Spleen and Stomach.

It also has the capability of working on the heart level and the spiritual level together, aligning to a more calm and deeper understanding of heart issues or spiritual journeying.

Herbalism is greatly enhanced with the energies of this stone, not only in its administration but also in the study of herbs and their actions.

Green Tourmaline is sometimes combined with Pink Tourmaline to produce the beautiful Watermelon Tourmaline – usually a darkish green wrapping around a pink centre. A delightful combination that really lifts the heart.

Because of the strong links of Verdelite with nature, if one chooses it can also bring one closer to the Devic world and Fairy Realms. These are part of the journeyings towards the True Source and these realms can assist in spiritual understanding because of their guardianship duties and links with the planetary elements, and the loving and capable part that these nature guardians play in nurturing and orchestrating the growth of all things around us.

Keywords for Verdelite are: Heart Balancer, Prosperity, Nature.

45. Yellow Jasper

Jasper is a form of quartz called Chalcedony, and is generally red, yellow or brown though sometimes it comes as green. It can also be multi-coloured and even look like a piece of artwork when the layers of color combine or collide.

Jasper is associated with relaxation, contentment, compassion, nurturing, consolation, tranquility, completion, wholeness, healing and gentle endings.

Jasper has often been used to help with dream recall and shamanic journeying. It is also a stone of protection and absorbs all types of negative energies.

Jasper facilitates in balancing and aligning the physical, mental and emotional bodies.

It is a stone of strength, courage and determination.

Jasper stimulates creativity and imagination, encouraging ideas into action. It can really assist people who need more focus, organization abilities, and motivation. It is also said to be good for protection from radiation.

Yellow Jasper is a protective stone, which can shield you against negativity and depression. It is said to channel positive energy increasing feelings of well-being and building self-confidence.

Yellow Jasper is also thought to provide protection to the traveler and to those working with the spirits. It can also be used to help relieve travel sickness.

The colour yellow is associated with the Solar Plexus Chakra and Yellow Jasper will stimulate and balance the Solar Plexus Chakra. Balancing this Chakra can help to reduce feelings of stress and anxiety.

When used in healing work, Jasper is recognised as the "supreme nurturer" as it holds and supports a nurturing and grounding energy during times of stress, bringing a sense of completeness and tranquility.

Yellow Jasper is also believed to energize the endocrine system, release toxins and to aid the stomach and digestion.

All jaspers work in a subtle way to give slow and gentle healing.

Yellow variety works well for the stomach, intestines, liver and spleen areas. It is very effective for grounding and often has an Earthy feel to it.

Each color of Jasper has additional specific qualities when used alone. Jasper works particularly well in conjunction with Opals. It is often recommended for executives as an aid to quick thinking. It also assists in helping them to endure stress.

Green Jasper is related to the Respiratory System and the Heart Chakra.

Other related properties are its ability to aid in the following: General tissue regeneration, mineral assimilation and general healing.

Darker colors of Jasper tend to be more grounding.

Because it will not over-stimulate any part of the body, it is often recommended to be used for gem elixirs.

It is generally considered to be more effective if it is used for long periods of time because it works slowly. It is a methodical and meticulous worker.

Jasper is very beneficial to the endocrine glands and the cleansing organs, and tends to make one feel stronger and in better physical condition.

Keywords connected with Yellow Jasper are: Its benefit to the Aethereal Fluidium, "Supreme Nurturer", Travel Stone, Order.

New Crystal Codes

The New Crystal Codes

Evolving Crystals

As the Earth's frequency changes, so too does the capability of crystals, born of her sweat and tears.

The link between earth and crystal cannot be overlooked. The planet has been undergoing many changes, and has been faced by so many threats that now includes the clearly visible environmental and energetic damage done by mankind in many ways.

We are also moving through time and space in an unprecedented way.

Some of the proven ways that worked before still work, however, they may well be limited now and need an upgrade.

Since 2001 there have been many revelations regarding these upgrades in how we use and process energy. With the various indications by the turnover of the clock of tick-tock-time into the new millennium and with the predictions according to the Mayan Long Count Calendar, many things have changed in the perceptions of countless consciousnesses around the globe.

New technology has brought us a plethora of information. Some good, some bad.

We have been dealing with shifts in so many areas, and just as within many of us latent codes and memories are resurfacing, often having been triggered through the energetic actions of the shifts both on the Planet and off it, so too this is impacting on the very makeup and matter of this our Earth.

As the planet is evolving, all beings and creation are being given the opportunity to evolve, or to devolve.

The crystals of today are come of age.

The codes laid down long ago, born of eons of trial, labour and action, are now revealing themselves as never before.

They are ready to be awoken.

Their messages are waiting and wanting to be heard.

Vortex Energies

You may have come to an understanding by now that as we spiral through the Cosmos, we are creating a kind of vortex of our own... And this is so, to a degree.

The vortex energies that we are working with here are not just these energies. We are moving from the simple firing backwards and forth in a crystal, the "time-keeping" and stabilizing to a certain frequency, if you like, offered by crystals and their previous innate actions.

We are now accessing the Vortex actions not only within the Cosmos, but also within the crystal!

Their energetic possibilities can now more fully embrace this cosmic spiraling action.

The consciousness and *awareness* of the spiraling action, even though it has been present for a long time, is the key to accessing and using it. There often has to be a build-up, a climax of consciousness for a tipping point to reach a new platform or level. And we are reaching it.

As human understanding can, for some, evolve to bridge other dimensions, so now the same opportunity is afforded to crystals. If you are working on a 3D issue that has other dimensional 4D or 5D issues, frequencies, disresonances and blocks, harnessing the new potential with your crystal can assist you to break through these dimensional blocks and bring a deeper healing to the situation.

WHAT ARE THE CRYSTAL CODES?

Crystals carry codes. Codes are a way of passing information on that does not rely on word or picture. Codes can also be a way of protecting information. Codes are a way of bypassing the intellect, and of initiating a program or macro-program. Codes can initiate a single program or a sequence of them.

With the advent of the book and movie on the DaVinci Codes and the interest in the esoteric, the secret and the occult, it is not surprising that more are beginning to have an interest in things unseen and previously hidden to us.

There is much hidden information in symbolism – the media and those attempting to inform and instruct us in a subliminal and hypnotic way use codes of colour, shape, placement, frequency and ambiance.

Many societies, governing orders, even secret organisations utilise codes in a variety of ways.

We have our own sets of codes, more commonly in our physical make-up – in our DNA and genes. And we have our own codes within our consciousness and conscience, within our heart even.

There are codes all around us if we could only be aware of them. Some can help, some can hinder.

The codes in nature, in crystals, in essential oils do not have agendas other than to assist us.

The codes in crystals are amazingly effective... as they are all based on Light frequencies and Energy... yet they use a variety of programs and frequencies to create and store their data and messages.

Generally the crystals will impact their resonance toward the crystalline body that is present in all humans, and they can impact and affect human energy systems, including the chakras, the aura and energy fields, the meridians, the nervous system and even down to the skeleton.

Certain crystals may also be programmed to act on other crystals in a similar way, sending out messages and data that activates the crystalline structures of other crystals – this is called resonance.

Crystals can hold any of these codes. I have called them Cipher Codes. Some crystals can hold several different types of codes, each with its own data and particular 'program'.

Crystal Codes can also be held in colour, in their crystalline molecular formation, in the markings, windows and shapes though they are not necessarily dependent on a particular shape or colour, or a particular type of crystal window.

The codes are now working on several levels. If you let them. They will embrace and harness energies to bridge and heal not only 3D issues, but can help with those issues that have history grounded in (past or present) 4D and even 5D realms. Advanced conscious humans are finding themselves operating on more levels than just 3D.

Color Frequencies – Color Codes

Each color has an etheric vibration, an unseen color frequency that impacts upon our energetic frequency body in a particular way.

These unseen color vibrations create specific actions on the Etheric body, which is the underpinning or the scaffolding if you like of the physical matter, and the matrix for the energy bodies.

We have vitality, life-force, electrical and magnetic living energy in the body that can be monitored and measured in frequencies, and even photographed or tracked with electronic devices. When we take a look at this energetic subtle body anatomy, we become aware of the etheric makeup of the physical and unseen energy bodies that everyone possesses. Each level of energy, each system, each organ has its own frequency.

We are all familiar with clear crystal quartz, which at first glance can appear to look a bit like glass of some sort. This is usually referred to as Clear. Yet even quartz can be opaque and look like milky white. This then is referred to as White. Both have slightly different codes because of this.

But not all crystals are white or clear.

Crystals are a combination of Colours and these colours are codes of light, with shapes that channel this light, being of a molecular composition that further dictates its action, possibly containing hidden data that also provides certain frequencies that allow each to work in different ways.

The minerals that compose the actual crystal or gem is what gives it its colour. These minerals have an effect on the physical body as well as other energetic unseen aspects of the body and being.

For instance, if we don't have enough magnesium in our diets, this affects our ability to hydrate properly. This can cause faulty neurological and electrical signals in the nervous system and brain, as well as the kidneys which processes our fluids and mineral and chemical balance in the body. This in turn compromises correct function in the body and creates imbalance in how things work. Magnesium is a white powder and essential for the assimilation of Vitamins within the body as well as the function of a lot of physical processes.

Other minerals will have different effects – sulphur is yellow and is essential in small doses for healing. And so on...

No matter the actual colour of the mineral, the message is this; a crystal containing a particular mineral can assist in balancing the body if there is a deficiency or a problem with that same mineral. I am not saying this is the only way crystals work, not at all. I am suggesting that sometimes there is a correlation between mineral composition of a crystal and how it can affect us for the better.

There are certain general actions with crystals of certain colours, as a lot of the crystal books out there inform us. You may be able to become more aware of the expected effect when a crystal combines a colour, a shape, a molecular composition and a hidden Cipher code.

Crystal Colour Codes

Here is a guide to some of the attributes of the colour codes.

CLEAR – Transparency, Reveal and Expose, Cleanse

BLUE – Purity, Purify, Water, Recharge

DEEP BLUE – Calibrator When Opened, Sonic Pulses of Love and Light

GOLDEN YELLOW – Unity, Co-Operation, Creativity

GREEN – Harmony, Equilibrium, Nurture

MAGENTA – Spiritual Protection, Evolution, Expansion

MAROON – Ground, Protect, Earth Connection

OLIVE GREEN – Female Leadership, Reclaim Feminine Power Without Harm

ORANGE – Shock Healer, Joy Bringer, Emotional Healer

PINK – Harmony, Allowing Without Fear, Love Vibration, Inner Child Healing

PURPLE, VIOLET – Purify, Transform, Evolution

RAINBOW – Being In Uniqueness, Expression, Healing, Celebration

RED – Life Force, Vitality, Activity

TURQUOISE – Consciousness, Connection, Cosmos

TURQUOISE BLUE – Renewal, Transformation, Information

TURQUOISE GREEN – Growth, Detachment, Ego-Less, Community

WHITE – Cleanser, Calibrator, Consciousness Opener

YELLOW – Mental Cleanser, Clarity, Focus

BLACK – Protection, Grounding, Absorbing or Deflecting

CRYSTAL CIPHER CODES

Crystals can hold any of their codes in the form of markings, grooves, striations, strings, inner chinks, and apparent mal-formation. But they can also be energetically hidden in plain view in clear crystals of a certain quality or calibre.

Some crystals can hold several different types of codes.

The codes are not dependent on a particular shape or colour of crystal or a particular type of crystal window. They tend to hold their secret to themselves unless you seek to know.

Cipher Codes are programs in data form that already re-exist within your crystal. Similar to operating software, they can work with or even provide other hidden programs when recognition is given to their abilities. A computer does nothing until one knows how to switch it on and to access what it can do...!

The types of codes that we can find in a crystal are:

Activation Code

These are usually a set of codes that give specific sequence of instructions to activate a person's particular chakra or energy field in a specific way; or that give a set of vibrations to inform other crystals to awaken to an activation. The activations can be preset, to coincide with certain frequencies that we experience in our cosmic journey, or when a certain number of people attain a certain frequency within a certain distance of the crystal.

Consciousness Code

Karma has assisted in teaching many responsibility and growth. The Consciousness Codes are here to support the shift in consciousness of the individual, and through the individual the backup data codes running as secondary programs, assist the individual to emanate these codes to others, holding and supporting the shift with a steady stream of crystal consciousness. These crystals bring more of a different kind of light into one's world. Unseen things are revealed, and the truth becomes known.

Creation Code

Some beings on the earth now were here at the beginning. They undertook to assist and co-operate in the acts of creation, coming from many corners of the Cosmos. For some, they have had their creative abilities compromised through the karma of others by association, by projection or by other means. Creator Code crystals remember the original creation and they have been formed and formed over again by the eons. These vibrations remind past creator souls that they can again create. And that their creations are perfect exactly as they are. Healing is given, support provided, life begins anew.

Dormant Code

By their name you can see that these are codes that may have been dormant for a very long time. Issued with specific instructions they may well also have several sets of codes of macro-data that would be activated at the time of their emergence from their dormancy. The awakening or emergence can be triggered by another crystal of activation, or by a certain frequency that this Solar System passes through, or by the correct consciousness of the person working with it.

Dream Code

Many forms of data are contained in these codes. Their primary purpose is to melt the veils of fourth dimensional reality and other realities and memories, visions and futures through the practise of dreams. Dreamers are assisted when they work with a crystal that holds dream codes. Through the dreaming, they process and work. Some dreams may require further completions, and these codes assist the message to be heeded and concluded. With the dream codes, connections to the resources required is also vibrationally provided.

Earth History Code

Earth has a long history, and we are now recovering some of the lost or destroyed information of things that may be vital to our understanding and evolution. Crystals that carry these codes have been entrusted to keep faithful record of past events and to remind humanity of its past triumphs and its past mistakes. There may be accompanying memory activation of past life times, of past species on the planet or of past environmental disasters and faulty stewardship of the planet. And of the reminders of help that is on hand.

Evolutionary Code

Entrusted to assist with Evolution of the Planet or of those seeking a higher or spiritual path, these codes will remind those who have experienced initiations in past incarnations of their previous attainments and successes, particular in light of any current seeming failure or difficult challenge that they may be facing in their life. They may also impel those who have become "stuck" or forgotten why they were here, assisting them to get the lesson they have not quite understood yet so that they can move forward. It can also assist those who have had ancestral or family karma for several life times, and who are ready to "wipe the slate" and accept their own responsibility and leave others' responsibilities to themselves and their own soul journey. All of this assists the planet to evolve.

Genetic / DNA Code

We have an interesting past when it comes to human genes. Hominids: homo erectus, homo sapiens, homo sapiens sapiens and now the new and developing homo luminous. There is also a history in ancient scriptures of genetic imprinting by the "gods" that has created the human of today. Past genetic interference has regressed some genes and activated others that have dictated some of our current history and state. The activation of certain repressed DNA codes is now taking place, and some of our crystals hold activation patterns and programs. A delight to work with when they fall into your hands.

Healing Code

Where there is disresonance in a being's energy field, there will be an incongruence in what they desire or work to manifest. Crystals with Healing Codes are capable of clearing the disresonances that create misalignment of

Soul with heart, of mind with body, of doing with being. They help align values and priorities so that what one really seeks becomes aligned with how one goes about achieving it. Sometimes found in crystals with rainbows or water occlusions, and has been present in crystals containing another crystal within. They also often feel nurturing to the touch.

Instruction Code

The rare Instruction Code issues a specific message – unique to the data that has been coded in – for a specific action or intent to take place. This may not be conscious to the recipient, but it will be in alignment with the Soul Conscience of the person who it does become drawn to and to whom it reveals itself. Along with the instruction, there will be accompanying coded frequencies that will instruct and assist in synchronisation, the personal evolutionary growth to reach the frequency to complete the task, and the programs to assist with attracting the resources to do so. A mission indeed!

Planetary System Code

As part of the Cosmic Solar System group, Planet Earth has been journeying long. She has a consciousness of her place not only in the Solar System, but also in the Cosmic Group as a whole. She has a function within these systems, and these codes and code settings are vital to assist her journey. Many have been dormant or veiled, but these crystals are now coming to light and circulating the planet in the open again. They may initially look plain, and they tend to have rainbows or healed fissures. They are activated as soon as a light healer holds one and "sees" it.

Programming Code

Most crystals contain this, which is the ability to be programmed for heightened conscious utilisation of its given function. This is when we want to dedicate a crystal to perform within its abilities for a particular person, or a particular place. These can be changed, edited, and cleared or reset at any time.

StarSeed Code

The mission of the StarSeed Codes is to remind those StarSeeds amongst us of who they are, and of the resonances of their own true source. StarSeed Code crystals assist StarSeeds to hold their ground and provide them with memories and resonances of home. Over the eons, StarSeed dust from the Cosmos blown by the Cosmic Winds have arrived on planet Earth and their vibrations have often gathered into morphic resonance groups to bind together through planetary fusion into a crystal of uniqueness.

Synchronisation Code

As crystals are literally inbuilt vibratory receptors and broadcasters, it is not surprising that they have been chosen as the faithful and secret suppositories for the various advanced records appropriate to assist humanity on its evolutionary path. Timing is a vital function for a crystal and the crystals containing Synchronisation Codes intend to show us the art of being in the right place at the right time with the right people doing the right thing. Through this synchronisation, the planet is benefited as more order is brought into reality on several inter-dimensional levels, thus moving the planet into alignment with her own desire synchronisation. It contains huge access to many records and codes, including the Consciousness, Activation and Transmission Codes.

Transformation Code

The power of change within the bowels of the planet is translated and captured in the codes of Transformation. Specifically the ability to transform with the new frequencies that are presenting themselves today. Similar frequencies that were buried in Earth's past are captured, focused, channelled and re-translated into the specific messages and programs that help unleash new opportunities for growth with conscious learning and ease.

Transmission Code

Transmission codes in a crystal enable the crystal to receive transmissions that convey information. Sometimes these are individual messages to the carer and carrier of the crystal. Sometimes they transmit messages to the environment when activated and working properly. Sometimes their message is meant as a frequency message that works on the environment they are in. Transmission messages may have been programmed eons ago, or the crystal may be coded to receive and subsequently to broadcast messages as they are transmitted from a Cosmic centre by the Guardians of Earth.

Accessing the Cipher Code

There are several ways to access the code within the crystal.

You can meditate on it and ask it to show you which code or codes it contains. You can use a pendulum and test as you go through the list of Cipher Codes. You can use kinesiology to test for the relevant information. You can stroke it with your thumb or sleep with it under your pillow, and some of you that are able can dream on it.

Or you can journal on it. When I mention journaling, this is a process of holding the crystal in one hand whilst writing freely and in an unstructured way, almost like having a conversation, with the other hand, allowing information to flow through in a meditative state.

There are certain people who can simply pick up a crystal and intuitively know what it contains. And there is nothing stopping you from doing or trying this for yourself, and then checking it with a pendulum or one of the other methods above.

It is all up to you. And it is a pleasant surprise to have your 'sensing' confirmed.

If you don't get it right first time don't give up. Being open to hearing or sensing what is not immediately visible or manifest can be developed. The exercise can then become like a kind of training...

You can also ask your crystal to work with you, safely and elegantly, if inter-dimensional issues are attached to the concern you are working with. Having been aligned through the Alignment Process will make this easy.

The Alignment Process

The Alignment Process is in two parts:

How to align the self first.

How to align and activate your crystal to the new energies.

Alignment Process For Crystals

Crystals are evolving along with the planet and the potentials in human consciousness. Now is the time to realign crystals and the mineral kingdom with the New Incoming and Vortex Energies so that they may assist us in a new enhanced way and support the new demands that the current changes are making. It is all part of our evolution.

Simple Self Alignment First

To align your crystal is easy, however, you firstly need to align yourself.

Here are the instructions to do so.

Prepare to Align

Establish a clear space and place in which to perform your alignments. If necessary meditate beforehand. Otherwise, use clearing space sprays or whatever practice you use to know that you are centered, clear in intent and free from interfering energies from other sources. Some may chose to use a pendulum to ascertain the energies before and after your process. This is my chosen method.

If you already work with energy healing or affirmations or kinesiology, then you can simply use the following statements / affirmations to balance and set the energies. Otherwise, use a simple ritual with music, intent, or whatever you feel will work. There is no right or wrong, this is about pure intent and respect.

[For those of you who would like to know how to use kinesiology self-testing for yourself, please note that easy and step-by-step instructions are included in my book *"Secrets Behind Energy Fields"*.]

The three easy steps are–

1. Establish the current energy activity / pattern / flow
2. Align Safely to the New Energies
3. Activate the New Energies

Establish the Current Energies

We need to establish a benchmark – this is to see the current 'reading' in order to compare after alignment and activation to ensure that this has been completed properly.

Using a pendulum is often best and easiest for this, though I have included some statements / affirmations for you to test or activate with. We are only looking to see what currently *is* before we move on to aligning our self, and ultimately our crystal.

The intention is to establish the current or energy-frequency if you like that represents how your body energy is in harmony with the new cosmic and planetary energies. By this I mean simply find a way to see how your energy is registering – the pendulum may show that it is going backwards and forwards, or it is going from side to side, or it is going anti-clockwise. If using kinesiology, you may test to see how much percentage the statement is true.

This is not a test as to how good / clever / pure etc you are, there is nothing to prove here, it is simply a test to establish your current state, which may have possibly been affected by a variety of things, including life...

> *"I am 100% in appropriate alignment with the New Incoming planetary and cosmic Energies"*

– Test to see your current percentage – use a pendulum or kinesiology test to see what percentage is currently operating in relationship to you and your crystal. Take note of your reading / your result.

[**Note** on Percentage testing: When testing a statement that says "I am..." without adding the "100%" you only need to be 51% to get a "Yes" or positive response, which can be misleading, as a 49% reading would render a "No" response. Using 100% will surely show you when you are completely aligned.]

If you want to take the opportunity to pursue further or deeper where you are at currently, you can also test yourself for electromagnetic function:

> *"My electromagnetic field is in appropriate and self-supportive alignment with the Planet"*

To be fully in alignment with the planet is not necessarily correct and appropriate for *all* humans, as we each have a different history and a different soul journey and goal. To be in full alignment may mean for some that they take on some of the planet's personal journey energy and thus can be kept busy dealing with planetary issues, problems or karma that can impinge upon or possibly delay their own soul journey.

Alignment to the New Energies

Having established the current status, we now focus our attention. With conscious intent, state a full and correct alignment:

> *"I am now 100% easily and safely appropriately aligned with the New Incoming Energies in a way which supports me, my health, my growth, my Soul and my journey"*

When you are confident that this statement is now in effect and that any blocks to its truth are now cleared (sometimes only a little time is required in order for this to occur).

Activation of the New Energies

Now that you are aligned to the new energies in a way that supports you, you only need to establish that these energies are now activated. With clear focus and intent state:

"I now activate my ability to work with the New Incoming Energies 100% safely and easily. The New Energies now support me"

After you feel or sense that this has become a truth for you, and that any blocks to this statement have been cleared, you may retest the energy in the same way as when you first established them at the beginning of this process.

Notes on the Process

If you find that when testing with a pendulum your initial reading was a backward and forward motion or an anti-clockwise circular motion, and that it has now changed to a clockwise circular motion, you have successfully realigned and activated the energies correctly.

Now that your energies are aligned correctly, you can align and activate your crystals to the new energies.

Aligning and Activating your Crystals

Always ensure that your energies are correct and aligned first, as described above, before attempting to align and activate your crystals to the new energies.

Establish the energy motion of your crystal; as you did at the beginning with your own energy assessment, if you have a pendulum, test it for direction and motion.

If you're not sure how to do this, I find a simple **"Show Me what you are Doing"** will get the pendulum to respond and give you an indication of its motion or energy movement. The crystal will show you what it is doing energetically, what energy flow it is working with.

Again, the back and fro movement can mean that the energy is pretty static, and whilst possibly indicating a "Yes / No" in usual questioning circumstances, when testing for crystal energy flow, this motion will usually only indicate a stilted flow in the crystal. Anti-clockwise motion when indicated with a crystal usually means to me that it is not yet in current alignment, and not correctly activated. When it is in a clockwise circular motion, it is showing me that it is processing energy actively and correctly. It seems to me that it is indicating an energy flow from a kind of energy vortex that is in harmony with the New energies and the Planet.

If there is no movement, you know for sure that your Crystal really needs your help.

If this is the case, then as mentioned, it will need cleaning and clearing, followed by alignment and activation.

If your crystal has been totally shut down, you might also add the statement:

"This Crystal is now 100% free from all interference and negative energies and now healed and fully ready, willing and able to respond to energy"

When your pendulum or testing shows you that your crystal has processed this and is indicating energy movement again, even with just a simple backward or forward response, move on to activating and aligning.

The best statements that I have found to use for crystal activations are:

"I now 100% easily and safely align this Crystal to the New Incoming Energies"

"My Crystal is now 100% ready, willing and able to assimilate and work with the New Incoming Energies"

As I say this statement several times over (usually three times is enough) I also touch the crystal with the tip of my left hand index finger. This is simply because it is easier for me to use my pendulum to watch the energies shift and the pendulum to swing differently. It also allows for transference of my instructions energetically through this contact. For by touching the crystal you allow it to align to your new energies and awareness, and it will respond more quickly than just saying the statement.

"I now activate this Crystal's ability to work with the New Incoming Energies 100% safely and easily. The New Energies now support the Crystal and myself"

"I now work with my Aligned Crystal in new and more powerful ways easily and safely"

This statement helps to activate it to co-create and co-operate with you in a new and more evolved way.

You may also choose to make up some of your own statements to program your crystal with in light of what you now know.

I also noted that around the time of an Eclipse, the crystals had a kind of hiccup, and defaulted back to their old energies (pendulum swung backward and forward again instead of clockwise circular) so they just needed me to touch them again and declare:

"I am now fully realigned with the New Energies easily, safely and completely"

and they happily changed their energy motion as I watched the pendulum change to a positive circular or vortex motion again.

And that is all you need to do!

Your Crystal is now ready to assimilate and utilise the New Incoming Energies easily and effectively.

Do you notice a new kind of energy sparkle to it?

NOTE: As I have performed these activations and alignment in Australia in the Southern Hemisphere only, there may be a question as to which is the best motion regarding gravity and energy spiralling (as evidenced by water draining from basins differently in both hemispheres – clockwise circular vs anti-clockwise circular.

My sense is that it doesn't matter, and that the best action indicator is still clockwise for both hemispheres. This, of course, is only my opinion. But it does fit in with other understandings of energy actions of transformation that I am aware of.

The New Energy Waves

What is 'The New Energy Wave'

What do we *mean* by the term 'New Energy Wave'?

We are all aware of the force of gravity on our planet. We are aware of the power of solar flares to affect all our electrical equipment. Some of you are also aware of what can happen in delays or in creating communication problems when the planet Mercury goes retrograde approximately once every three months for about three weeks.

Well, right now the planet is moving through some interesting frequencies in space. There are a lot of planetary alignments that have not occurred for over 26,000 years, and as these planets move into alignment, they affect and so shift and change the normal movements of space winds, and the way of the electromagnetic relationships of the set paths of the planets.

This impacts on our world.

We are also experiencing shifts within our planet, such as global climate changes, increased weather pattern changes, increased earthquakes, tsunamis, and other natural phenomenon.

In short, we are experiencing changes both above, from outer space, and below, from the planet we stand upon.

And many of us are seeking new ways of riding these new waves.

As we move in space through and past the end-time of the *Kali Yuga* – which was indicated by and coincided with the Mayan Long Count Calendar which ended in December 2012 - and align with the *Galactic Center-Galactic Anticenter* axis - we experience new vibrations. These vibrations meet with our energy fields, and where there is resistance, they 'shake' up and attempt to integrate. When they cannot penetrate and flow through easily, we experience a variety of 'symptoms' or discomforts.

Many of us are evolving, and as we evolve, we reveal the new subtle body anatomy and specialized Chakra Systems that are enhancements to our current Major Chakra anatomy. This has been progressing for some time, as we move into the new and higher frequencies.

There is talk of 'Ascension', which may be helpful to think of as 'Upgrades' of our systems, frequencies and purpose, as well as our destination. This creates changes. This creates growth. With growth there is sometimes pain as we leave an old garment behind to don a new and better one. This is the process that many of us are in right now.

We are 'converting' - 'upgrading'... - quite possibly 'ascending'...

The myriad of new symptoms resulting from these conversions of our energy systems to the new and higher 'New Energy Wave' frequencies do not all lend themselves to resolution through some of the old methods and techniques. 3 Dimensional techniques help 3D issues, but we are moving into 4D and 5D frequencies – and in some cases some of you are already moving into other dimensions.

Maintaining balance within will assist us, as we are being forced to discover new arts of inner healing as we encounter and deal with the many changes surrounding us right now.

Where To Next?

Now that you have discovered the impact of the new incoming frequencies, and are also now able to utilise your recharged and revitalised Crystal more fully and effectively, what do you do next?

Working with the new energies will be a priority over the coming years for many. There are few that will not be impacted. Even those who are not interested in self development or in self responsibility will be impacted for no-one can avoid these incoming frequencies. We have the opportunity to evolve along with the energies or to begin a process of devolution or constriction.

Working with the Crystal Cipher Codes can be quite exciting, and allowing for the growth of our crystals through our conscious acknowledgment can certainly be a worthwhile endeavour. Next time you go shopping for a crystal, or pick one up to work with again, take a moment to acknowledge it and to allow it to reveal its hidden codes to you.

Evolving Chakras

I would like to mention the use of Crystals with the Chakras in consideration of the changing frequencies. The old premise of using certain fixed colours of crystals for certain chakras has been overturned, and we need to look at exactly what is required for the chakra at any given time. Time had shown that we use the colours of the Chakras to identify the colour of the correct crystal. However, this may lead to over-energising the chakra if the Chakra actually requires a different frequency and consequently a different colour to nurture and bring it back into balance again. Staying tuned to what a chakra requires is vital to correct alignment, balancing or healing.

As the Chakras evolve, tools to balance must also evolve.

For centuries we have worked with the Seven Main Chakras System; Base, Sacral, Solar Plexus, Heart, Throat, Third Eye and Crown, and we applied the colours from the rainbow in a way to match the understood colour of the Chakra. Red was used for the base, orange for the Sacral etc. and through to purple / violet. However this is all changing and some newer and higher vibrationary colours are now being required. There have also been changes in the Chakra system itself.

In relatively recent years we have discovered the Hara System and the Higher or Upper Chakra System. These work on a different Dimension than the main Seven Chakras which bridge 3 Dimension and 4 Dimension . We have also discovered the Evolved Earthing Chakra System which enables better grounding and inter-dimensional earthing of the new Higher Chakras as well as anchoring of the Seven Main Chakras. Further Chakra Systems have been revealed and are unfolding in many people's personal subtle body and esoteric anatomy. A new book about these is being completed, but until then you can read a little more about some of these new evolved systems on my website pages:

http://www.myrasri.com/new-chakras-subtle-body-anatomy

If you work with energy and wish to improve and enhance your work with others, then these may possibly be of interest to you.

For those of you who simply love Crystals and want to work primarily with yourself and with what you currently know, you will probably discover those of the new

Chakras that are important for you as and when you need to.

Whatever your path from here, I wish you well on your journey, for we each have our own journey and path to tread.

I wish you well, I wish you health, I wish you prosperity and peace. Blessings!

Thank you for sharing this journey with me.

Free Crystal Codes Summary Chart

You can download an A4 version of the following summary chart from:

http://www.myrasri.com/book-buyer-new-crystal-codes

THE NEW CRYSTAL CODES SUMMARY CHART

CIPHER CODES

1. Activation Code
2. Consciousness Code
3. Creation Code
4. Dormant Code
5. Dream Code
6. Earth History Code
7. Evolutionary Code
8. Genetic / DNA Code
9. Healing Code
10. Instruction Code
11. Planetary System Code
12. Programming Code
13. StarSeed Code
14. Synchronisation Code
15. Transformation Code
16. Transmission Code

COLOUR CODES

1. CLEAR – Transparency, Reveal and Expose, Cleanse
2. BLUE – Purity, Purify, Water, Recharge
3. DEEP BLUE – Calibrator When Opened, Sonic Pulses Of Love And Light
4. GOLDEN YELLOW – Unity, Co-Operation, Creativity
5. GREEN – Harmony, Equilibrium, Nurture
6. MAGENTA – Spiritual Protection, Evolution, Expansion
7. MAROON – Ground, Protect, Earth Connection
8. OLIVE GREEN – Female Leadership, Reclaim Feminine Power Without Harm
9. ORANGE – Shock Healer, Joy Bringer, Emotional Healer
10. PINK – Harmony, Allowing Without Fear, Love Vibration, Inner Child Healing
11. PURPLE, VIOLET – Purify, Transform, Evolution
12. RAINBOW – Being In Uniqueness, Expression, Healing, Celebration
13. RED – Life Force, Vitality, Activity
14. TURQUOISE – Consciousness, Connection, Cosmos
15. TURQUOISE BLUE – Renewal, Transformation, Information
16. TURQUOISE GREEN – Growth, Detachment, Ego-Less, Community
17. WHITE – Cleanser, Calibrator, Consciousness Opener
18. YELLOW – Mental Cleanser, Clarity, Focus

CRYSTAL SHAPE CODES

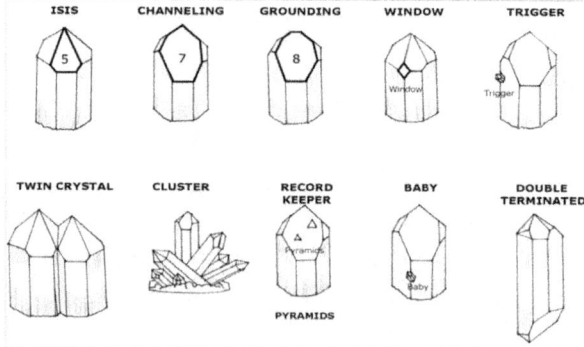

CRYSTAL STATE

- CLEANSING REQUIRED
- CLEARING REQUIRED
- PROGRAM CLEARING
- REPROGRAM
- MAINTAIN
- ALIGNMENT OF CRYSTAL

Myra Sri ©

Further Information

Sources and Acknowledgments

"Crystal Handbook" - Kevin Sullivan

"Love is in the Earth" – Melody

"The Book of Crystals" - Fiona Toy

"The Crystal Bible" by Judy Hall

"The Complete Crystal Guidebook" – Uma Silbey

About the Author

Myra Sri was born in England and moved to Australia in her twenties with her then husband and two young children. As a highly sensitive person, she maintained a spiritual leaning.

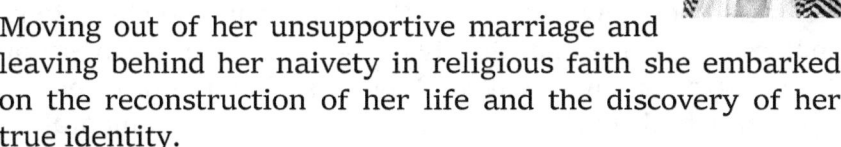

Moving out of her unsupportive marriage and leaving behind her naivety in religious faith she embarked on the reconstruction of her life and the discovery of her true identity.

Continuing to work in the mainstream business, accounting and media industries, she found that connecting with other people further inspired her on her own self development journey and assisting others in their journeys led her to naturally gravitating to the healing professions.

Undertaking extensive training and study she became an energy healing practitioner and kinesiologist. Qualifying as an instructor in several modalities, she subsequently discovered where there was a lack of teaching and understanding and set upon research and discovery, resulting in her own unique advanced workshops which have been taught around Australia since the early 1990's. These continuing experiences led her to develop her own innate skills and supported her in re-membering her healing skills and psychic abilities.

Running her own private practice since the late 80's, Myra remains an avid explorer and student of evolving ways to heal and support the soul and spirit.

She wrote her first book in 2006. Regular trips to the UK concerned family issues until both her parents died and after further teaching and training in England and Germany Myra returned to Australia being freshly inspired to document and write about her new learnings, discoveries and insights, including the current energy shifts since the turn of the millennium affecting essential oils and crystal energies as well as the emergence of the new evolved Chakras.

She embarked on the Energy Healing Secrets Series in 2012 which fulfils part of her role as a Transformation Agent. The Energy Healing Secrets Series is presented to assist in self help, self healing and spiritual mastery.

With the advent of the new era energies and her discovery of the new evolved Chakra systems, she has written and developed the *New Evolved Chakras Workshop series* which includes the new Earthing Chakras, the Psychic Body Chakras and the Signal-Survival Chakras. The discovery of these extraordinary Chakras have also been confirmed by other spiritual teachers and psychics to be instrumental in everybody's healing process and the book on these Chakras is soon to be published.

Myra provides a safe and attentive healing space for her clients and students, and works multi-dimensionally, enabling major energy and spiritual shifts. Her focus is on the Soul and spirit. Considered a resort for difficult or complicated situations, she has often been referred to as 'the Healer's Healer'. She works multi-dimensionally, enabling major energy and spiritual shifts.

Some of Myra's workshops include:

- Past Life Training – Navigating Soul Journey and Genetic Issues and Karma safely

- HygienEthics Series (Protection and Energy Management Series) – Working With Energy, Living With Energy, Being Energy, Protection HygienEthics, HygienEthics for Therapists, Advanced HygienEthics

- Navigating Life in a Changing World

- Muscle Testing Basics

- Crystal Workshop

- New Evolved Chakra Series - New Earthing Chakras, New Psychic Body and Chakras, New Signal-Survival Chakras

Contact Information

Thank you for taking the time to read this book. Please feel free to write to the Author with your success stories. Your questions are welcomed and every endeavor will be made to answer each one.

As an Author and fully qualified Kinesiologist, Spiritual Coach and Healer, Trainer and Instructor, Transformation Agent, and Vibrational Energy Healer Myra intends to pass on her specialized information and knowledge to assist others in their journeying.

If you would like more information about this or any other book or meditation or to be kept informed of the publication of the New Evolved Chakras book, you can email her direct, or register your email for newsletters at www.myrasri.com or follow Myra at her Amazon Author page – http://www.amazon.com/author/myrasri

Email: admin@myrasri.com

Websites: www.myrasri.com   www.newevolvedchakras.com

FREE NEWSLETTER:

Get the free newsletter which lets you know when there are special deals and offers, new meditations and books, as well as current news items on life, challenge, change, self help healing, self empowerment and spirituality.

Sign up obligation-free here: www.myrasri.com

Other Books by the Same Author

Energy Healing Secrets Series

Secrets Beyond Aromatherapy

Secrets Behind Energy Fields

Secret Truths to Health and Well-Being

Secrets to Serene Space – Space Clearing

Guided Meditations at www.myrasri.com/shop

Latest Book:

The New Evolved Chakras – New Era Chakra Balancing and Alignment

Books Due For Publication Soon:

The Sensitive's Guide to the Psychic Sensory Chakras

Affirmations

Stay tuned to my website www.myrasri.com for future publications or you can simply register your interest by signing up for my newsletter.

SECRETS BEYOND AROMATHERAPY

The beauty and power of Essential Oils has been known to us for thousands of years, from Ancient Indian healers to current day aromatherapists.

Few were aware of etheric Colour Codes of Essential Oils.

Until now!

Essential Oils, like the Chakra systems, have evolved and Come of Age.

Their abilities have expanded and they are now poised ready to assist us all as we work with and move fully into the new energies of this new Era.

Come on a journey into the astounding colours of oils; see how they interact with human senses and subtle body anatomy. Learn their impacts and the unseen implications with the Soul and incarnational aspects. Discover which Chakras respond best, and which energy system is most enhanced by their actions. You may be pleasantly surprised!

The basic etheric body colours of the human energy systems appeared to have undergone change. Even the Main Chakras are responding differently to colour and vibration. It would seem that no longer do most of us reflect (and often poorly at that) the basic opaque paint-box-type colours previously associated with the seven basic colours of the rainbow – some of us are now able to reflect more glorious and colourful hues and iridescences from and through the auric layers and chakras when balanced correctly.

Living in cities can prevent some of these new hues and their tints from shining within and without, as the electromagnetic smog and pollution can lower the frequencies to a paler and poorer version. In these times it is becoming more important to reconnect back to nature, the land or the sea, purer energies, higher vibrations and natural remedies whenever and wherever possible to sustain us. And the essential oils is are part of this remedy.

The humble oil along with knowledge of its inherent etheric colour codes and abilities will further enhance everyone's experience of the nature and the knowing that is held within each loving oil and hidden within the etheric world itself, and will further enhance and amplify all of your current benefits when used with the increased awareness.

Recognize the New Roles that these amazing gifts from our Planet are playing right now.

Explore the Etheric Colours of over Thirty Essential Oils. Learn their Secrets.

Find new and powerful ways of working with them.

Spend time with them. Let your choice of Oil reveal to you further hidden information to assist you with your client or with your own personal transformation.

Work with Essential Oils in ways you've never done before!

Amazon Reviews:

A treasure of energetic information

Thrilled with the content of this book and I have read almost every aromatherapy book there is

I wonder why this book is not used as a textbook

SECRETS BEHIND ENERGY FIELDS

When we have good health, we really do have a huge asset at the ready – there is no price to be placed on it as from our good health so many positive things can arise. When we are exhausted and tired through dealing with other people's issues, emotions and energies, we are cheating ourselves of our true destiny and life journey.

Nobody lives as an entire isolated and energetic island to themselves. We are all social beings and part of life is social interaction of some kind or another. Which also means energetic interaction - the contact that takes place on those unseen levels, yet we can still feel their action and their impact.

When we don't know where our energy goes, when we work with others closely, when we are faced with emotional or traumatic scenes, when others think it is ok and acceptable to explode around us, when we think there must be something wrong with us because of what we continually encounter in our life, we need answers to what is happening, and what we can do about it!

Learning to navigate through life in energies that are less than positive or harmonious sometimes requires outside information or help. And all you really need to invest is some of your time and energy to become your own energy guru and healer.

Here is a collection of techniques, exercises and tools that are proven energy strengtheners. Selected from the many workshops I have taught on this topic are easy, effective solutions and understandings for anybody who is involved with other people and not coping as well as they could.

You can begin to reclaim your own identity and autonomy again, and easily recognise who and what has been affecting you with the easy to follow instructions and ideas.

Be successful and happy, protect your energy and let good health and good energy be your positive foundation.

SECRET TRUTHS – HEALTH and WELL-BEING

If you are doing everything "right" and yet there is something that cannot be explained that compromises your experience of life and vitality, you may well need to look deeper... look past symptoms, past the apparent, past expecting a pill to fix what you can do for yourself.

Exhaustion and tiredness can have several causes. Compromised health can often find us resorting to the local doctor or our health food store. Energetic and emotional impacts, toxicity or damage from others may need to be addressed and resolved separately ("*Secrets behind Energy Fields*").

We are not just our body, we are not just our mind, we are not just our emotions. We are an amazing combination of all of these and more. The being is an amazing orchestration of matter and that unseen life-force; spirit. When one part is hurt, the other parts are affected.

Here in this book we look at important and often hidden contributors to compromised health and vitality as well as very real yet often hidden aspects of tiredness, exhaustion and depletion of energy. Many are not aware of simple things that one can fix for oneself. Nor how easy it can be to make a few mental or verbal changes for oneself that creates a positive impact on health outcomes.

If the nervous system is compromised by amalgam fillings, or lack of hydration, or unresolved issues, then results will be way short of what is possible. If the mind is blocked through lack of simple yet essential nutrients, and is not even aware of essential requirements for health, if a person cannot recognise when they have adrenal exhaustion and how their thoughts can feed into this, what chance does one have of full recovery? If inflammation is causing pain in your body can you do anything about it?

Here is a mix of experiential physical advice and of energetic and spiritual tips from a long-standing expert on body-mind-spirit issues, written to help those who wish to find answers to their problems or symptoms on the *physical level* themselves.

SECRETS TO SERENE SPACE

A new look at the Art of Space Clearing. Clear Negative Energies and Use Metaphysics to Change Your Space and Life. Become your own Guru. Learn the Art of Creating Sanctuary, within and without…

A home is a place to return to for safety, nurturing, rejuvenation and love. Does your home sanctuary nurture and support you? Does it fill you with pleasure and enjoyment?

Take a moment to look around your home… how does it reflect you? How does it feel to you? Are you able to revitalise and rejuvenate there whenever you need to? Does your home welcome you? If the answer is "No" and you are aware that you need to do something to change your space, and possibly yourself, then you will find lots of ideas and help in this book.

If you want to go deeper than just shifting surface stuff around, if you feel that there could be some old "nasties" lying around somewhere that you would like to shift, if you feel that you would like to get clearer within yourself as well as within your living space, then this is the book for you!

Decluttering may be needed. Or it could be that there are some old or negative energies to clear. What about the sense of being "spied" on? Learn about how to remove not only "nasties" but also learn what a Portal is and how to clear these, as well as Orbs and Thoughtforms. Discover not only how to Clear your place and enhance your home and life, but the crucial and essential step that must follow for true and lasting success in your Clearing.

Here in an easy to read book you will find how to create Sanctuary in your own personal space with time-proven tools. Decluttering is made easy. Imprints are explained and removal instructions are included together with further powerful techniques to incorporate into your ritual or chosen exercise to bring healing into the home.

This is a true self help book!

SECRETS Beyond Aromatherapy

CHAKRA HEALING SECRETS
ETHERIC COLOUR CODES
TRANSFORMATION SECRETS

Behind the Invisible Etheric Codes
of Essential Oils
Chakra and Energy Healing Secrets
for the New Era

MYRA SRI

Secrets Behind Energy Fields

BECOME YOUR OWN ENERGY GURU
RECLAIM YOUR ENERGY & VITALITY

MYRA SRI

SECRETS to SERENE SPACE

E CLEARING
E ENERGIES
SICS AND
O CHANGE
D LIFE

SECRET Truths Health & Well-Being

HEALTH TRUTHS THAT EVERYONE SHOULD KNOW
TOXICITY AND THE NERVOUS SYSTEM
SECRETS BEYOND NUTRITION

Resolve Exhaustion and Tiredness NATURALLY!
Recognise Obstacles to Health and Vitality
Body-Mind and Emotional Impact

MYRA SRI

The NEW CRYSTAL CODES

Align Your Crystals
To The New Energies

CRYSTAL CODES, CIPHERS AND FUNCTIONS
FOR THE NEW ERA
New: ALIGN YOUR CRYSTALS
CHOOSING AND WORKING WITH CRYSTALS

Learn the difference between an SJL, a Record Keeper, a Lemurian
and more Stone...
Sets of crystals to assist in love, success, protection, life stress

MYRA SRI

www.ingramcontent.com/pod-product-compliance
Lightning Source LLC
Chambersburg PA
CBHW050532300426
44113CB00012B/2056